Should You

BUY THIS BOOK?

60 PREPOSTEROUS FLOW CHARTS TO SORT YOUR LIFE OUT

Published in Great Britain in 2019 by
Carlton Books Ltd
20 Mortimer Street
London W1T 3JW

10 9 8 7 6 5 4 3 2 1

Project designer: Emily Clarke
Project editor: Chris Mitchell
Designer and illustrator: Sam James
Illustrator: Lee Bruce

A catalogue record for this book is available from the British Library

ISBN 978-1-78739-169-7

Printed in Dubai

Should You BUY THIS BOOK?

60 PREPOSTEROUS FLOW CHARTS TO SORT YOUR LIFE OUT

JASON WARD

INTRODUCTION

When he was still the President of the United States, and we were all so much younger, Barack Obama only wore blue or grey suits. "I'm trying to pare down decisions", he explained in a 2012 interview. "I don't want to make decisions about what I'm eating or wearing because I have too many other decisions to make."

This is just one of the many things you have in common with Barack Obama*. As can be testified by anyone who has spent so long trying to decide what film to watch that they've run out of time to watch anything, an excess of options is paralysing. Every day brings an endless series of choices, and making them is exhausting even when their consequences hold negligible geopolitical significance.

To counteract the fatigue of being alive, then, here is a modest attempt to answer almost every question you might face in your near-to-long-term future, from "Is that milk in the fridge still okay to use?" to "Should you take a job as a nightwatchman at that creepy abandoned fairground (which closed down in mysterious circumstances following a series of unsolved murders)?" This might or might not prove helpful, but will at least pass the time until you have to decide what to make for dinner, and the agony can begin all over again.

*You also loved *The Wire* and I believe in you.

CONTENTS

CHAPTER 4: WORK, WORK, WORK, WORK, WORK, WORK

CHAPTER 5: HOBBIES! ART! MOVIES! LITERATURE! VIDEOGAMES! MUSIC! PUNCTUATION!

CHAPTER 6: THE FUTURE

INDEX

CHAPTER 1

Who are you?

IN A PERSONAL SENSE, I MEAN.
I DON'T WANT YOUR LIFE STORY

ARE YOU A BAD PERSON?

SCANDALS

Are you dedicated towards your goals?

It's my dream to open a nightclub across the train tracks called "Scandals".

Are you passionate about the Arts?

Yes, I keep applying to be a contestant on *The Apprentice* even though they've told me to stop.

The lead single from my Christmas album became deeply unpopular after tabloid revelations that I had stolen both the melody and lyrics from the Color Me Badd song "I Wanna Sex You Up".

Take it up with the songwriter, who I am legally obliged to state is definitely not me.

Across any train tracks.

How do you like to have fun?

But that song doesn't have anything to do with Christmas.

Neither does "Baby, It's Cold Outside" but you still hear a creepy new cover version every couple of years.

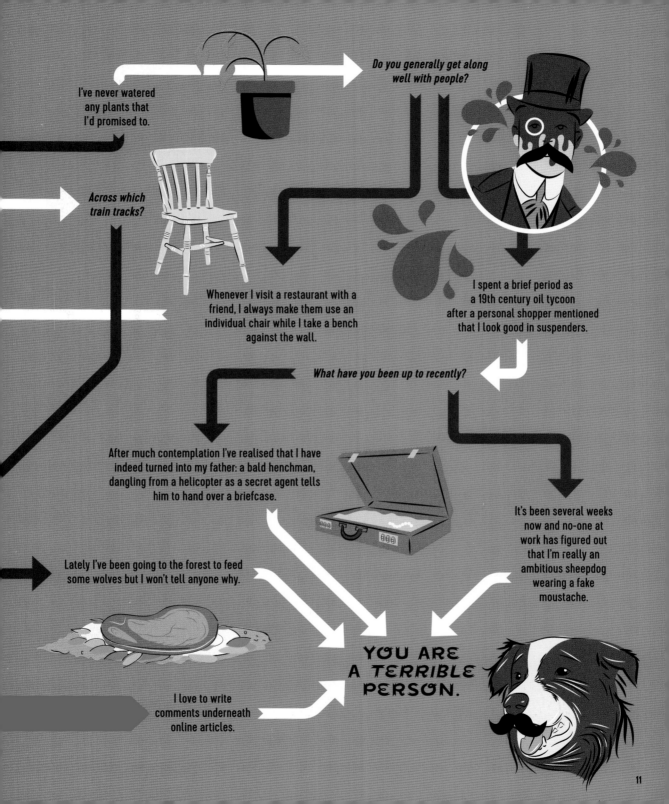

I've never watered any plants that I'd promised to.

Do you generally get along well with people?

Across which train tracks?

Whenever I visit a restaurant with a friend, I always make them use an individual chair while I take a bench against the wall.

I spent a brief period as a 19th century oil tycoon after a personal shopper mentioned that I look good in suspenders.

What have you been up to recently?

After much contemplation I've realised that I have indeed turned into my father: a bald henchman, dangling from a helicopter as a secret agent tells him to hand over a briefcase.

It's been several weeks now and no-one at work has figured out that I'm really an ambitious sheepdog wearing a fake moustache.

Lately I've been going to the forest to feed some wolves but I won't tell anyone why.

YOU ARE A TERRIBLE PERSON.

I love to write comments underneath online articles.

WHICH DAY OF THE WEEK ARE YOU?

Are you able to wake up in the morning without hitting the snooze button forty times?

YES

NO

Do you sometimes feel like baking a cake, even though it isn't a special occasion?

YES

Will you cross the street just to get a better look at a cute dog?

YES

NO

Do you fancy getting a drink after work?

YES

NO

You're
MONDAY.
Wow. You had an 85.71% chance of getting something else and you still ended up with Monday. Monday! Where do you get off?

You're
TUESDAY.
I'm not going to lie to you – Tuesday is pretty bad. You are not going to a party on a Tuesday. You are not going to fall in love on a Tuesday. You probably won't even have anything interesting for lunch on a Tuesday. Sure, you're not Monday, but that's like saying that at least you're not as bad as the very worst person you know.

You're
FRIDAY.

They don't usually specify, but it's a fair bet that most pop songs — excluding the ones about heartbreak or ascertaining which individual let the dogs out — are set on a Friday. Even if the full promise of a weekend is rarely fulfilled, it doesn't matter: the future always seems warmer with you around.

You're
THURSDAY.

While you're generally well liked, it's telling that there is absolutely nothing else to say about you.

YES

NO

I know it's 16:00, but let's make some last-minute plans for tonight!

NO

YES

You're
SUNDAY.

Despite your easy-going exterior, you're actually pretty complicated. You regret not making more out of yourself recently and yet, against your own experience and better judgement, you remain generally hopeful of what lies ahead. You are either too hard on yourself, or not hard enough.

Does the idea of doing nothing all day except watching an entire season of a TV show in your pyjamas sound like a genuinely valuable use of your finite time on Earth?

Z Zzzzz

NO

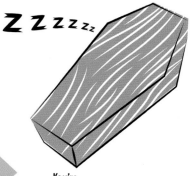

You're
WEDNESDAY.

It's hard to say whether Wednesday is a mediocre Friday or an over-performing Monday. If you choose to take this as me saying that you're either a good version of something bad or a bad version of something good, then that's your prerogative.

You're
SATURDAY.

Sure, Saturdays sound great, but according to folklore it's the only day that vampires aren't allowed to leave their coffins, leaving them vulnerable to attack. So really it depends on whether you're undead or not. I'm trying to insinuate that you're not to everyone's tastes.

WHO WERE YOU IN A PAST LIFE?

Let's start with the basics:
Do you believe that you were someone else in a former life?

YES

NO → Do your friends regularly ask you to cut their hair?

NO

Are you a fan of early rock 'n' roll?

YES

NO

YES

NO

Have you got an affinity for leeches?

Have you ever felt drawn to visit Sun Studio in Memphis, Tennessee?

YES

YES

NO

Do you often have a compulsion to eat cheeseburger after cheeseburger, possibly while wearing a spangly jumpsuit?

Are you fundamentally indecisive?

NO

YES

YES

I'M NOT SURE

You were
AN ELVIS PRESLEY IMPERSONATOR.
Sadly, the statistics are against you. Many have tried on the sunglasses and sideburns, but there was only one King, baby.

You were
A BARBER SURGEON.
In the Middle Ages it was common for hairdressers to moonlight as surgeons, and you should know. Maybe you grew up wanting to help others, maybe you just owned a really good bread knife. I wouldn't advise giving it a go now, though.

You were
A SKEPTIC PHILOSOPHER.

A bit of a head-scratcher, this. In a previous life you were apparently a philosopher who spent their entire career attempting to refute the concept of reincarnation, which is precisely the sort of notion that such an individual would have dismissed as bunkum. It's odd, but the results – like an apocryphal six-year-old George Washington, or Shakira's hips – don't lie.

You were the
PRESIDENT OF THE UNITED STATES.

Before you get too excited, I should mention: yes, you were once the President of the United States. More specifically, you were Richard Nixon, disgraced 37th President and all-round deadbeat. Well done… I guess?

NO

YES

Do you enjoy spending long periods of time in the garden, doing very little?

YES

Do you have an inexplicable phobia of tape recorders?

Have you ever wanted to grow a really, really long beard?

NO

You were
A SERF (PROBABLY).

I'm sorry, it's not very sexy, but there are over 100 billion dead people and almost none of them cured polio.

YES

NO

You were
AN ORNAMENTAL HERMIT.

Unbelievably, 18th century aristocrats actually used to pay people to dress as druids and live in their gardens full-time. This, I'm afraid, was once your profession. At least until your job was stolen by a ceramic gnome.

You were
A BAKER.

They had bakers in the past too, of course. You were very happy.

WHICH BODY OF WATER ARE YOU?

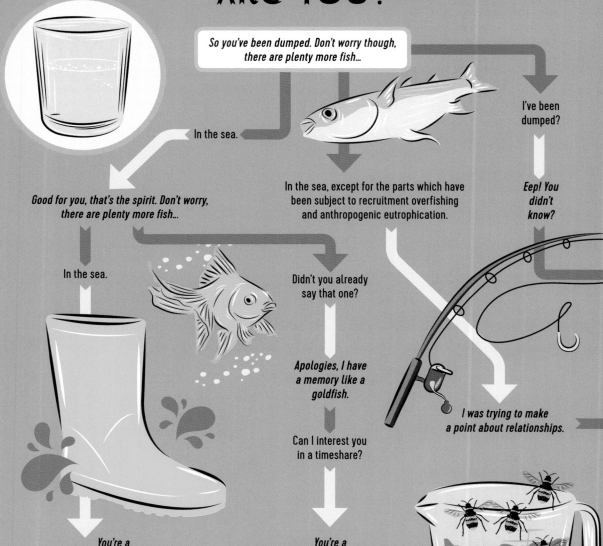

So you've been dumped. Don't worry though, there are plenty more fish...

In the sea.

Good for you, that's the spirit. Don't worry, there are plenty more fish...

In the sea, except for the parts which have been subject to recruitment overfishing and anthropogenic eutrophication.

I've been dumped?

Eep! You didn't know?

In the sea.

Didn't you already say that one?

Apologies, I have a memory like a goldfish.

Can I interest you in a timeshare?

I was trying to make a point about relationships.

You're a
PUDDLE.
Let's face it, you're a little shallow. No-one is going to mistake you for a lagoon or a mangrove swamp, but don't fret: every ocean started life as a puddle. That isn't actually true, but you'll believe anything. You're basically a bit of rain lying in the street.

You're a
RESERVOIR.
Is your bad reputation deserved? Yes, people are in undeniable danger when they tangle with you, but that's hardly your fault. You're useful but unsafe, like a measuring jug filled with bees.

You're an OXBOW LAKE.

It happened so gradually that you didn't notice it. Once you were vital, flowing, alive. You weren't just a bend in the river, you were the river. But things changed, and here you are. Left behind. Sooner or later the river changes course for everyone, you suppose, yet you never thought it would actually happen to you. You were the river, after all.

Strewth!

You're a BILLABONG.

Yes, you're an oxbow lake too. You're just Australian and have a better name.

STILL WATERS RUN DEEP.

Ugh.

...   ...   Yes?

This is awkward. I just wanted to assign your personality to a body of water.

Sorry, I didn't realise you were sensitive. I suppose...

Are you planning to stop with the sea-related idioms any time soon? I'm genuinely upset.

I mean, I knew we were having trouble, but I thought it was just a blip.

It's alright. Worse things have happened at sea!

sobs uncontrollably

You're a LOCH.

Underneath your placid surface lies hidden depths – depths that may conceal a Plesiosaur or other supposedly-extinct Sauropterygian marine reptile from the Mesozoic Era. But depths nonetheless.

And I'm trying to make a point about effective fishery management.

17

WHO IS YOUR NEMESIS?

Have you been feeling for a while that you are in some way cursed, and that this isn't just bad luck – it's as if there's some twisted form of poetic justice behind the highly specific miseries that now regularly befall you?

Also, have you ever committed a hit-and-run while driving over the moors on a foul, moonless night?

YES

NO

Do you find yourself getting into arguments with strangers at self-service checkouts?

Have you ever been coaxed into a local swimming pool and then found your reflection so entrancing that you eventually died and turned into a daffodil?

Your nemesis:
PROBABLY THAT WITCH YOU RAN OVER.

YES

NO

Your nemesis:
YOU

There are other possible answers here, but you always knew, somewhere deep down, that this was coming. After all, if you run into jerks all day, you're probably the jerk. The only thing in your own way is you, as Rocky said in that movie. No, not <u>Rocky</u>, the new one.

Your nemesis:
THE HEAT DEATH OF THE UNIVERSE.

YES

Do you ever feel a crushing sense of sincere hopelessness at the idea that life is a finite blip, and that every person on the planet right now will be dead in 150 years, and by then – your life long forgotten – it will be as if you never existed?

NO

Your nemesis:
THE ALWAYS-THERE FEAR THAT YOU'RE NOT QUITE ALIVE ENOUGH.

NO

NO

NO

Do you mutter "typical" whenever a train is late, even if this happens pretty rarely in relation to the number of trains you take?

YES

YES

Would it also feel typical for you to end up with a nemesis almost at random?

YES

In an extraordinary and baffling coincidence, your nemesis is literally
THE GREEK GODDESS OF RETRIBUTION CALLED NEMESIS.
You also ran her over.

Your nemesis:
THE DUTCH,
for reasons you'll never quite figure out.

WHICH MOON IN THE SOLAR SYSTEM ARE YOU?

Would you take a long walk to try out a new café even though your regular one is just around the corner and the new café might be awful?

YES | **NO** →

You're THE Moon.

If the Moon was an ice cream – and I know the point of this paragraph is that you're the Moon, but stick with me here – then it'd be vanilla: enjoyable, yes, but a safe and somewhat obvious choice. Also it's named after the actual thing that it is, which would only be appropriate if it orbited a planet called Planet.

If this new café was indeed awful, would you continue going there anyway out of some perverse need to stand out?

NO →

YES

Would it change your mind if I told you that certain parts of the café reach temperatures of 1649 degrees Celsius?

You're Deimos.

People may tease you for being the smallest moon in the solar system, but don't worry: in Greek mythology you personify dread. What's more, at only seven miles in diameter, if you were ever colonised then every person living on you would have an acceptable commute to work.

NO

YES

You're Triton.

Unlike the other major moons, Triton orbits in the opposite direction to its parent planet. This may explain your stubborn refusal to own a smartphone, even though you have no qualms about asking friends to look up directions, bus times and the filmographies of assorted character actors for you.

You're IO.

I'm just going to come right out and say it: you're hot. By which I mean that you have 400 active volcanoes on your surface and it's probably impossible to buy a fan anywhere near you.

20

WHAT'S YOUR SECRET IDENTITY?

I've heard you've decided to fight crime,
but why do you need to conceal who you really are?

I'd like to be free from accountability, the constraints of local law
enforcement and a democratically-sustained judiciary.
Also I love to play dress-up.

I'm afraid that my burning sense
of injustice would put my loved
ones in perpetual danger.

Would you like your secret identity
to be <u>so</u> half-hearted that you look
virtually identical to the way
you did before?

Would you be able to get a job at
the Louvre and not have anyone
immediately notice that you're an
anthropomorphic reptile?

YES

NO

Are you willing
to learn
shorthand?

NO

YES

Your secret identity:
**MILD-MANNERED
REPORTER,**
glasses wearer.

YES

Your secret identity:
CURATOR OF
ANTIQUITIES,
definitely not an immortal
Amazonian princess.

NO

Your secret identity:
**BILLIONAIRE
PLAYBOY,**
horrible person.

Your secret identity:
**MUTANT
TURTLE**
wearing a trench coat and
hat, hoping for the best.

WHAT'S YOUR GREATEST WEAKNESS?

How would you spend a perfect Friday night?

A nice dinner out with friends.

A glass of wine and a long soak in the bath.

I don't know, by Friday I'm exhausted.

What's your favourite thing about winter?

When it's over.

On a freezing day, seeing my breath plume out in front of me and feeling that life can be pretty romantic.

How beautiful a city can seem during the final months of the year — all lights and commotion and people dashing around in scarves and big coats.

Getting drunk and **LOOKING AT YOUR EX'S SOCIAL MEDIA.**

You've lost **EVERY PAIR OF GLOVES** *you've ever owned.*

WHEN YOU'RE IN A PUBLIC SPACE *and a member of the waiting staff drops something you feel compelled to yell*

"**WHAAAAAY!**"

A DIMINISHED SENSE OF SMELL.

How have you been
taking care of yourself?

You always misspell the word
"RHTYHM*"
on your first try.

I've been making an effort to write
regularly in my journal so that years from
now I'll be able to look back at this time
and remember what I did and how it felt.

I'll get around to it,
everything's just really
hectic right now.

These days I'm a lot more
thoughtful about my body, and I try
to look after it better.

I'm trying to be more comfortable
being alone and spending time
enjoying my own company.

Is there anything
you're proud of?

YOUR SUSPICION THAT YOU HAVEN'T BURNED YOUR BRIDGES

so much as you've allowed them to fall
into disrepair and now they can't
be crossed.

I'm a romantic
at heart.

Your acute fear of your

DENTIST'S INEVITABLE DISAPPROVAL.

I'm good at avoiding
conflict and letting go
of things even when they
bother me.

YOU'RE WAITING FOR SOMETHING

that happened years ago.

Don't you mean,
"Is there anything of
which you're proud?"

PRETENDING TO BE OKAY

with something then passively aggressively
bringing it up every chance you get.

PEDANTRY.

*Rhythm**

23

WHAT SORT OF
EGGS ARE YOU?

Well, you bought or borrowed (or plundered, you abominable miscreant) this book in an attempt to find out the answers to the big questions in life. And here we are, solving every single one of them. You're very welcome. Anyway. Do you enjoy riding the teacups at theme parks?

YES

NO

What about the Waltzer, or the Tilt-A Whirl? Before you say anything, I know they're all basically the same, I'm just doing due diligence here.

NO

YES

Ever fallen asleep with your head in a microwave?

NO

YES

Are there entire years of the 1960s that you are no longer able to recall?

NO

YES

You're Scrambled.

YES

You're Fried.

YES → You're Soft-boiled.

Do you usually spend longer running a bath than actually sitting in it?

NO →

Are people intimidated by the very idea of you, believing you to be much more difficult than you know you really are?

YES

You're Poached.

NO

Do you run a private detective agency on the mean streets of the roughest part of town, surviving on a diet of coffee, bourbon, cigarettes and danger?

YES

You're Hard-boiled.

NO →

You're an Omelette; *that's what you get for not taking part.*

WHERE WILL YOU BE IN FIVE YEARS?

| What do you think is currently missing from your life? |

FUN

EXCITEMENT

STABILITY

CAREER ADVANCEMENT

I don't know about you, but your family and friends will be gathering to commemorate the

FIFTH ANNIVERSARY OF YOUR MYSTERIOUS DISAPPEARANCE

after you ratted out that mob boss.

In the

WITNESS PROTECTION PROGRAMME,

fooling nobody.

In a wholly unexpected turn of events, a drunken Bradley Cooper will recognise your prodigious musical talents and everything will just get

BETTER AND BETTER

from there. Unrelated: the author of this book may not have seen the second half of A Star Is Born.

PLAYING CARDS
in the belly of a whale.

LOST AT SEA,
in all senses of the word.

You'll be almost
EXACTLY WHERE YOU ARE RIGHT NOW,
except for the eyepatch.

ADVENTURE

FAME

FIREWORKS
– literal ones, held slightly too close to your face.

FINANCIAL SECURITY

PEACE AND FRUITFUL SEASONS

You will become so wealthy that you'll take to
SLEEPING ON A PILE OF MONEY;
this will prove grimier than anticipated and you'll soon withdraw from public life in order to combat a debilitating series of paper cuts. Post-recovery, you'll attempt to dive into a vault of gold coins, Scrooge McDuck-style, and will never be heard from again.

Starting to wonder if the
ANNUAL BLOOD SACRIFICES
to appease the Norse god Freyr were the best business strategy rather than, for example, applying for an agricultural subsidy.

3,000 years hence, what remains of your skull will be found
BURIED DEEP IN RIVER MUD
by a hobbyist who will at first believe it to be a shard of pottery.

CHAPTER 2

Vitally important questions

AND ONE ABOUT WI-FI PASSWORDS,
BY THE WAY NO REFUNDS

IS THAT MILK IN THE FRIDGE STILL OKAY TO USE?

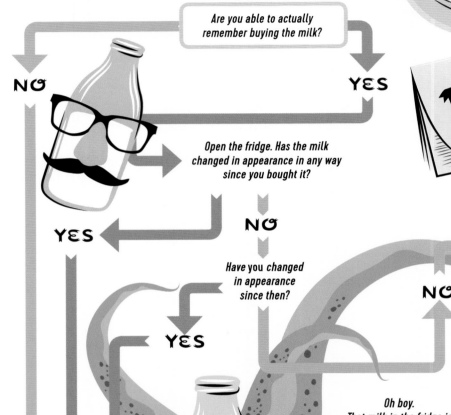

Are you able to actually remember buying the milk?

NO

YES

13 FRIDAY

Open the fridge. Has the milk changed in appearance in any way since you bought it?

YES

NO

Have you changed in appearance since then?

YES

NO

That milk in the fridge is NOT STILL OKAY TO USE. Step away from the milk.

Oh boy. That milk in the fridge is NOT STILL OKAY TO USE. Also you've apparently kept it so long that it's become an entirely new lifeform, so you might want to think about a cleaning rota.

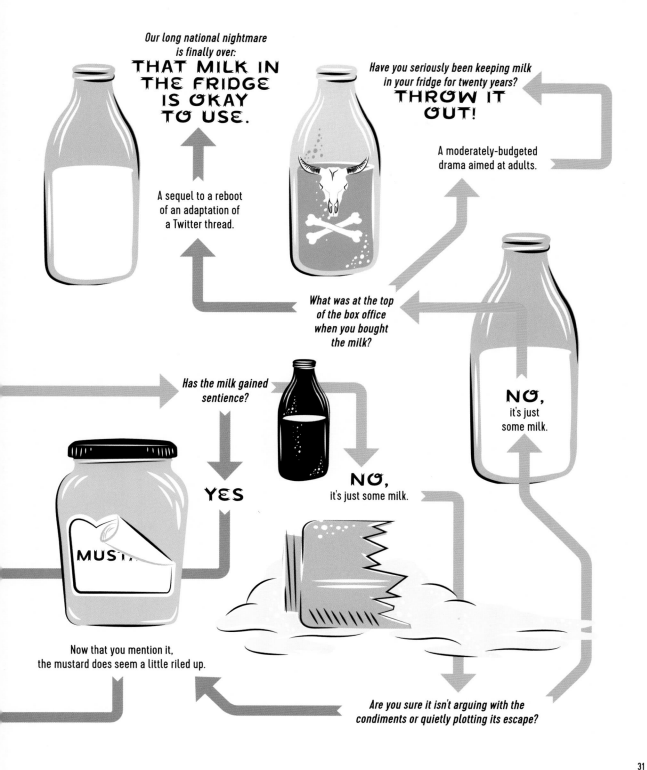

Our long national nightmare is finally over: **THAT MILK IN THE FRIDGE IS OKAY TO USE.**

Have you seriously been keeping milk in your fridge for twenty years? **THROW IT OUT!**

A moderately-budgeted drama aimed at adults.

A sequel to a reboot of an adaptation of a Twitter thread.

What was at the top of the box office when you bought the milk?

Has the milk gained sentience?

NO, it's just some milk.

YES

NO, it's just some milk.

Now that you mention it, the mustard does seem a little riled up.

MUST

Are you sure it isn't arguing with the condiments or quietly plotting its escape?

ARE YOU LIVING IN A
HAUNTED HOUSE?

Does your home have stairs?

YES

NO

My dog has started barking at things which aren't there and refuses to enter the utility room.

How are your pets?

That sounds suspicious, but what's more likely: that you're sharing your home with a spirit who has unfinished business in your utility room, or that you're sharing your home with a dog who's afraid of tumble dryers?

My cat is emotionally distant and acts like it's better than me. So it's basically the same.

FLAT 664

FLAT 665

FLAT 666

FLAT 667

But we don't have a tumble dryer...

I suppose you're right.

You have a
NEUROTIC
DOG.

As your home only has a single storey, it wouldn't be typically described as a house. You are living in a
HAUNTED FLAT,
or "apartment" if you're American. I'm glad that's all cleared up.

YOUR HOUSE
IS HAUNTED
but it seems to be localised to your utility room, so maybe just hand wash your clothes from now on?

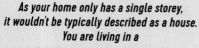

How about you – has anything unusual happened lately?

I've been receiving yachting magazines in the post. I don't own a yacht.

You're being haunted by

THE GHOST OF A WRETCHED MARINER

(or maybe an 80s businessman?) and they're really starting to take liberties with your home.

Yes, all of a sudden they'll seem deeply troubled and the colour will drain from their face.

I keep having bad dreams that wake me up at exactly 3am, but I can never remember what happens in them.

What's the temperature like?

It's fine, except for one spot that's always freezing cold no matter the weather.

Do visitors make excuses to leave soon after they enter your home?

Only when objects move around for no apparent reason.

It's fine; to be honest I'm more concerned by the walls pulsing with ectoplasm.

Do you often switch on the light in your living room and catch a chilling glimpse of two figures in clothes from an earlier century, tussling over a knife?

YOUR HOUSE IS HAUNTED.

Also you need to bleed your radiators.

Yes, but I have a horrible personality.

They are from the 18th century but I think it's a dagger rather than a knife, does that count?

Not often, but it's definitely happened a couple of times.

PUT SOME WORK INTO YOURSELF,
c'mon.

NOPE,
that'll just be a trick of the light.

I'm stumped.
IT'S PROBABLY FINE?

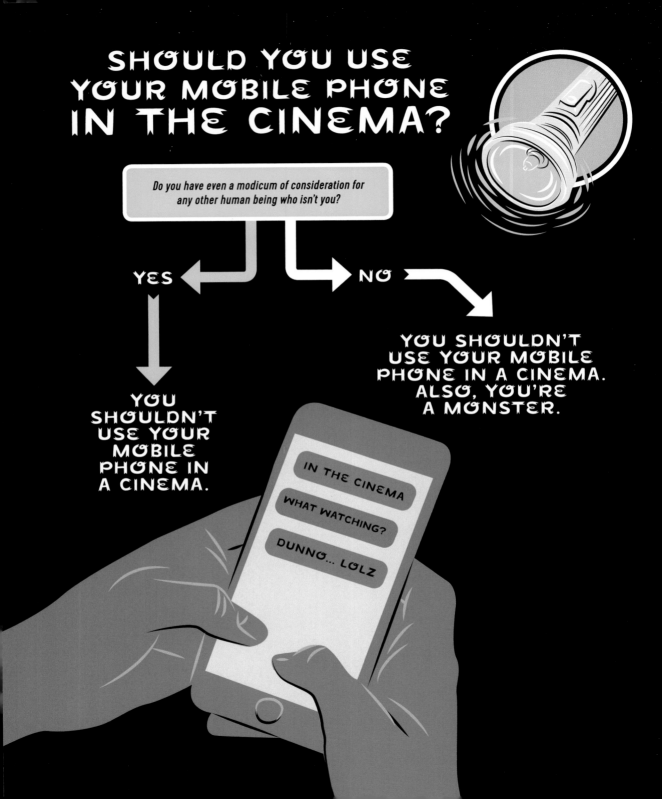

SHOULD YOU STICK YOUR ARM OUT OF THE BUS WINDOW?

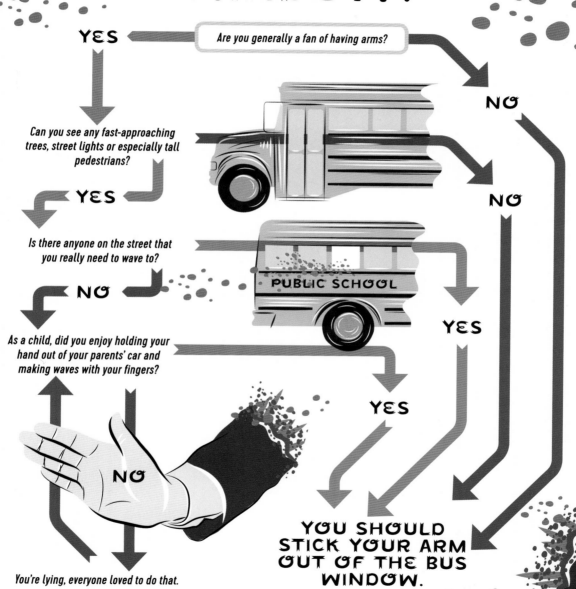

YES

Are you generally a fan of having arms?

NO

NO

Can you see any fast-approaching trees, street lights or especially tall pedestrians?

YES

Is there anyone on the street that you really need to wave to?

NO

YES

As a child, did you enjoy holding your hand out of your parents' car and making waves with your fingers?

NO

YES

PUBLIC SCHOOL

You're lying, everyone loved to do that.

YOU SHOULD STICK YOUR ARM OUT OF THE BUS WINDOW.

WHAT SHOULD YOU USE AS A WI-FI PASSWORD?

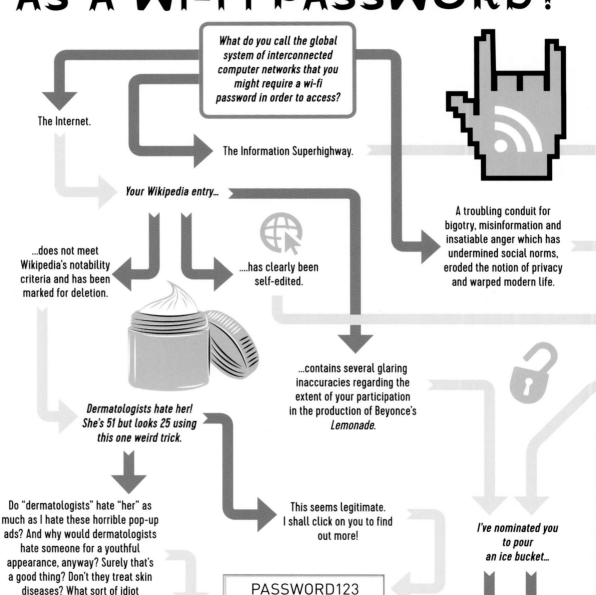

What do you call the global system of interconnected computer networks that you might require a wi-fi password in order to access?

The Internet.

The Information Superhighway.

Your Wikipedia entry...

A troubling conduit for bigotry, misinformation and insatiable anger which has undermined social norms, eroded the notion of privacy and warped modern life.

...does not meet Wikipedia's notability criteria and has been marked for deletion.

....has clearly been self-edited.

...contains several glaring inaccuracies regarding the extent of your participation in the production of Beyonce's *Lemonade*.

Dermatologists hate her! She's 51 but looks 25 using this one weird trick.

Do "dermatologists" hate "her" as much as I hate these horrible pop-up ads? And why would dermatologists hate someone for a youthful appearance, anyway? Surely that's a good thing? Don't they treat skin diseases? What sort of idiot would fall for this?

This seems legitimate. I shall click on you to find out more!

I've nominated you to pour an ice bucket...

PASSWORD123

TheOnlyTh1ngStrong3rThanMyCynicismIsMyPassw0rd

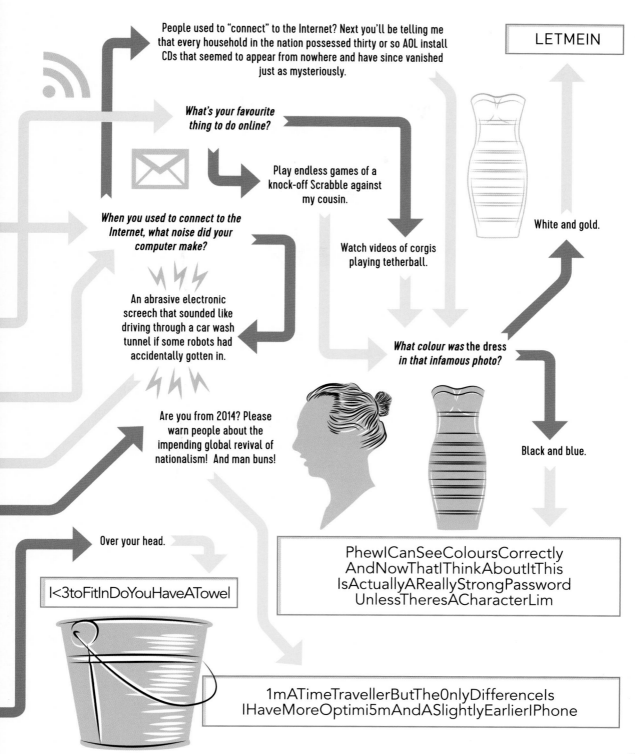

People used to "connect" to the Internet? Next you'll be telling me that every household in the nation possessed thirty or so AOL install CDs that seemed to appear from nowhere and have since vanished just as mysteriously.

LETMEIN

What's your favourite thing to do online?

Play endless games of a knock-off Scrabble against my cousin.

When you used to connect to the Internet, what noise did your computer make?

Watch videos of corgis playing tetherball.

White and gold.

An abrasive electronic screech that sounded like driving through a car wash tunnel if some robots had accidentally gotten in.

What colour was the dress in that infamous photo?

Are you from 2014? Please warn people about the impending global revival of nationalism! And man buns!

Black and blue.

Over your head.

PhewICanSeeColoursCorrectly AndNowThatIThinkAboutItThis IsActuallyAReallyStrongPassword UnlessTheresACharacterLim

I<3toFitInDoYouHaveATowel

1mATimeTravellerButThe0nlyDifferenceIs IHaveMoreOptimi5mAndASlightlyEarlierIPhone

37

YOU'RE LOST.
WHAT SHOULD YOU DO?

Don't worry, I'm going to help you get through this.

Thank you so much — I think I took a wrong turn a couple of streets back.

The most important thing to do is to START PANICKING.

AHHHHHH!

Are you sure that's right?
That sounds...
that doesn't sound right.

Sure it is. Your mind works faster when you're afraid.

Um, okay.
There's a river nearby, maybe I should follow that?

What's in your pockets?

My phone and wallet.

My car keys.

Terrific. Throw them in the river!

Really?
But wouldn't I nee-

Trust me!

Are you absolutely certain?

Hey, I'm here to help.

Alright, I've thrown my stuff in the river.
What should I do now?

Excellent, great work.

There's someone in a uniform coming towards me.
They're asking if I'm okay.

Oh boy: now there's a group
of angry-looking men
coming towards me.

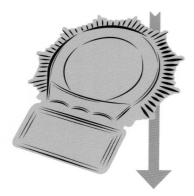

*How lucky! What you need to do now is tell them
that you're not from around here but you're holding
lots of cash – you know, in case they're afraid of you,
to let them know that you're a respectable sort.*

*This is going to sound alarming
but that's a trap.
Run away as fast as you can.*

If you're sure...

...

How did
it go?

Hello?

...

I DON'T KNOW
*– that's why I got you to throw everything
away. Your mind should be working super
fast now. Good luck!*

I GUESS THE GANG
MUST HAVE HELPED.
Another problem solved! I am <u>crushing</u> these questions.

WHAT **OBSOLETE CURRENCY** ARE YOU?

Are you a numismatist?

What's that, a type of obsolete currency?

Sorry, it's not my thing. Oh! I like early 80s New Wave and cereal grains, if you have any questions along those lines?

YES

It's the name for a coin specialist. You really know nothing about this topic?

Fine. What's your favourite song from Spandau Ballet's third album?

Are you trying to embarrass me? I didn't realise this book *of flow charts* had such a stringent barrier for entry. You're a regular Cecilia von Heijne.

TRUE

I absolutely know who Cecilia von Heijne is and am not about to quickly change the subject.

You're the **BUKHARAN TENGA,** and as you're such a currency expert I don't need to explain to you why, right?

OKAY

I can't believe that's true. You're **SHINPLASTER.** You were worth so little that people would actually add starch and water to you and use you to warm their socks.

Do you like rice, and I mean, <u>really</u> like rice?

GOLD

NO

YES

You're the **RYO,** a unit of Japanese currency which was equivalent to the amount of rice needed to feed one person for a year (assuming they'd be happy with the same meal 1,095 times in a row, obviously).

You're the **RHENISH GUILDER.** Admittedly, you hold very little importance to the German monetary system of the 14th and 15th century, but your love of gold provides you a kinship with the Rhenish gold guilder.

WHICH ANIMAL SHOULD YOU CHOOSE AS A PET: A KITTEN OR A CRAZED AUSTRALIAN SALTWATER CROCODILE?

Are you allergic to dander?

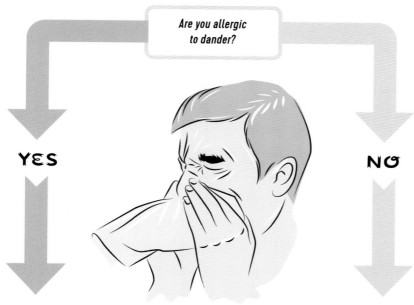

YES

NO

You should get a
CRAZED AUSTRALIAN SALTWATER CROCODILE.
Why put yourself through nasal congestion?

You should get
A KITTEN,
I guess.

YOU'VE JUST FOUND AN ENCHANTED LAMP. WHAT ONE WISH SHOULD YOU MAKE?

Ooh, how many wishes do I get?

Is there anything that your heart desires?

Have you ever heard of any actual person in the real world being given the opportunity to instantly have anything that they'd like? Something is happening to you that has never happened anywhere before, ever, and you already want more.

A sandwich, to be honest.

It's not even noon.

Okay, two sandwiches.

How is that better?

How many wishes though?

One wish. It's right there in the title.

Three is the classic amount.

Yes, in fictional stories read to children. You get one wish: go.

Well I can have one now and one for lunch.

Just the two sandwiches would be great, cheers.

I could give you a live-in chef to cook you incredible meals for the rest of your life. Or a button that makes dessert appear right in front of you. Or a drawer that's always filled with lasagne!

In that case I wish for no wishes.

Wow. Fine. What fillings?

Your wish is my command: here are two cheese and tomato sandwiches.

Your choice.

Oh.

What's wrong?

YOUR WISH IS MY COMMAN-
No wait, what?

You're just going to have to pick the tomatoes off, alright?

I'M GOING TO MY LAMP.

Nothing. It's fine. I mean... I'm not a huge fan of tomatoes, that's all. Can I change my wish?

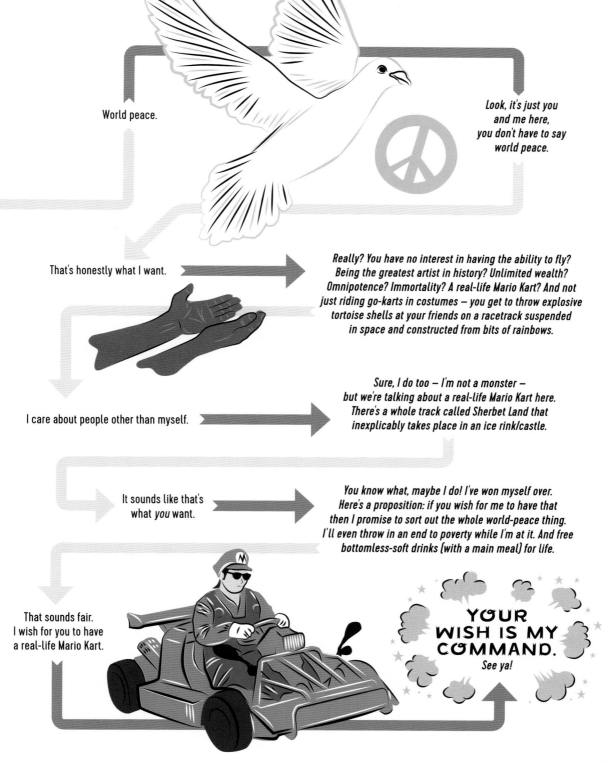

World peace.

Look, it's just you and me here, you don't have to say world peace.

That's honestly what I want.

Really? You have no interest in having the ability to fly? Being the greatest artist in history? Unlimited wealth? Omnipotence? Immortality? A real-life Mario Kart? And not just riding go-karts in costumes — you get to throw explosive tortoise shells at your friends on a racetrack suspended in space and constructed from bits of rainbows.

I care about people other than myself.

Sure, I do too — I'm not a monster — but we're talking about a real-life Mario Kart here. There's a whole track called Sherbet Land that inexplicably takes place in an ice rink/castle.

It sounds like that's what *you* want.

You know what, maybe I do! I've won myself over. Here's a proposition: if you wish for me to have that then I promise to sort out the whole world-peace thing. I'll even throw in an end to poverty while I'm at it. And free bottomless-soft drinks (with a main meal) for life.

That sounds fair. I wish for you to have a real-life Mario Kart.

YOUR WISH IS MY COMMAND.
See ya!

DID YOU LEAVE THE IRON PLUGGED IN?

Is there a nagging sensation in the pit of your stomach, as if you've forgotten something important?

YES

NO

Do you get this feeling every time you leave the house?

NO

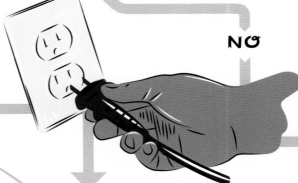

Do you remember leaving the iron plugged in?

YES

YES

Have you left the iron plugged in at any point in your life?

NO

YES

NO

YOU MAY HAVE LEFT THE IRON PLUGGED IN.

The only way to make sure is to ditch your friend's wedding and check.

YOU PROBABLY HAVEN'T LEFT THE IRON PLUGGED IN.

The stove on the other hand...

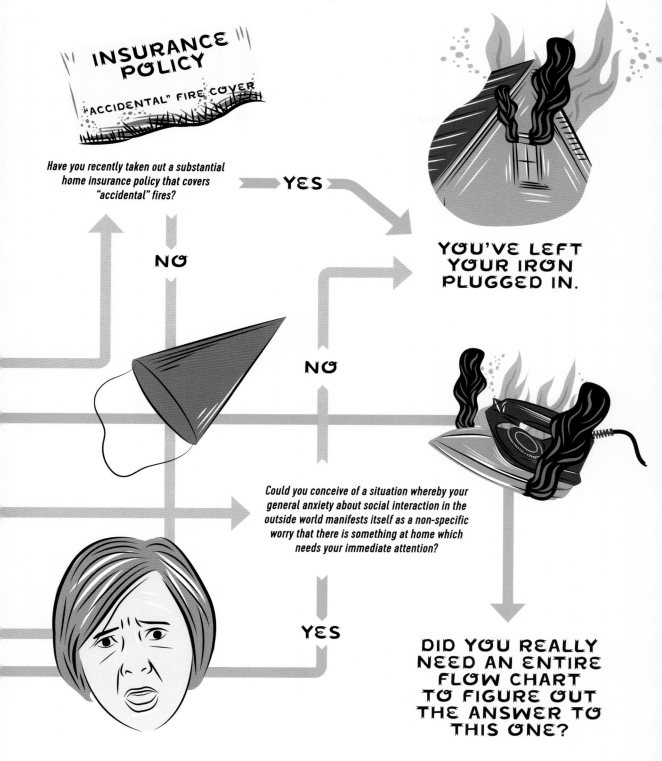

INSURANCE POLICY

"ACCIDENTAL" FIRE COVER

Have you recently taken out a substantial home insurance policy that covers "accidental" fires?

YES

NO

YOU'VE LEFT YOUR IRON PLUGGED IN.

NO

Could you conceive of a situation whereby your general anxiety about social interaction in the outside world manifests itself as a non-specific worry that there is something at home which needs your immediate attention?

YES

DID YOU REALLY NEED AN ENTIRE FLOW CHART TO FIGURE OUT THE ANSWER TO THIS ONE?

CHAPTER 3

Love

(AND OTHER TERRORS)

SHOULD YOU BREAK UP?

Does your romantic partner respect your beliefs, interests and career ambitions?

YES

NO

Are they entangled in the deadly yet seductive world of illegal street racing?

YES

NO

When you're around your partner do you feel like you're able to truly be yourself, for both good and bad? Do they "get" you?

NO

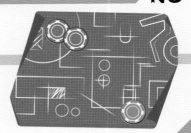

YES

YES

On date night, have they ever stood you up so they can conduct an elaborate casino heist?

NO

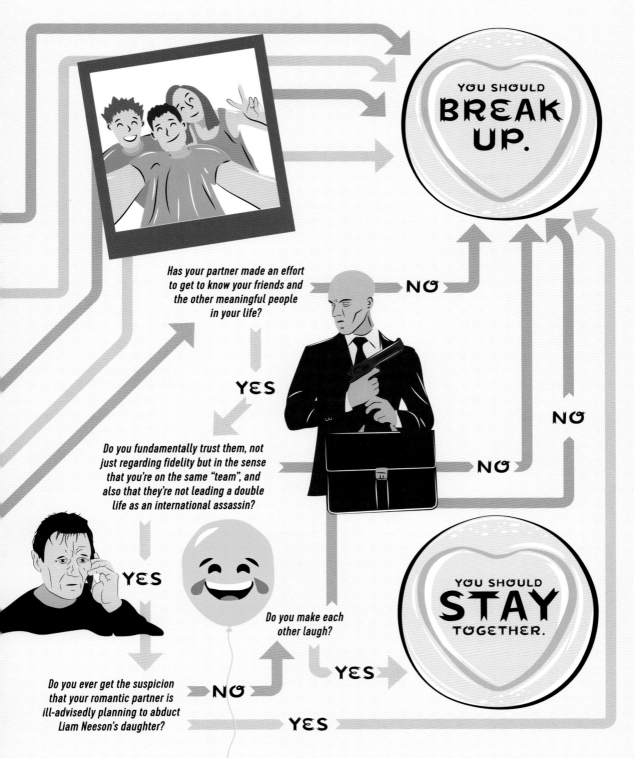

YOU SHOULD **BREAK UP.**

Has your partner made an effort to get to know your friends and the other meaningful people in your life?

NO

YES

Do you fundamentally trust them, not just regarding fidelity but in the sense that you're on the same "team", and also that they're not leading a double life as an international assassin?

NO

NO

YES

YOU SHOULD **STAY** TOGETHER.

Do you make each other laugh?

YES

Do you ever get the suspicion that your romantic partner is ill-advisedly planning to abduct Liam Neeson's daughter?

NO

YES

49

WHAT MONSTER IS HIDING IN YOUR WARDROBE?

Would you rather be buried alive or run over by a haunted lawnmower?

Buried alive.

Run over by a haunted lawnmower.

Would you rather be eaten by the Zombies – as in the 60s British Invasion group, not reanimated corpses – or for the surviving members of the Beach Boys to burn you to death inside a substantial wicker effigy?

Burned by Beach Boys (probably Mike Love's fault).

Eaten by (the) Zombies.

THE WOLF MAN.

Sure, with his fangs and claws and tendency to menace villages in South Wales, the Wolf Man is pretty frightening. But frankly I'd be more worried about him molting all over your clothing.

COUNT DRACULA.

No need to fret – the wardrobe reminded the Prince of Darkness of his coffin and he promptly fell asleep.

Would you rather be accosted by a washerwoman spirit who washes the clothes of those about to die, or to transform into a throw cushion every time there's a full moon?

NO-ONE.

Phew! You're safe; there isn't a monster hiding in your wardrobe.

Unfortunately, this is because they're actually under your bed, and they're <u>ready</u>.

Handwashing harbinger.

Lycanthrowcushionpy.

Double trouble.

Would you rather have a massive gorilla hurl barrels at you on a construction site, or for your dog to become significantly more successful than you?

Would you rather discover (and subsequently be sacrificed by) a hidden ancient civilisation, or meet (and be swiftly murdered and replaced by) your own doppelgänger?

Dog jealousy.

Ape peril.

Unwise rousing.

THE INVISIBLE MAN.

Well, he <u>was</u> in your wardrobe. He may have gone for a stroll by now, who can tell.

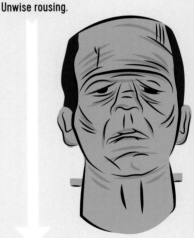

KING KONG.

You're probably doomed, but fair play: it's impressive that he managed to squeeze into such a tight space.

FRANKENSTEIN.

Don't worry, I know: Frankenstein was the name of the doctor, not the monster. But wasn't Victor Frankenstein really the monster all along, etc.? Either way, you should know that there's a Genevese scientist currently hanging out in your wardrobe. When I last checked he was fiddling with your clock radio.

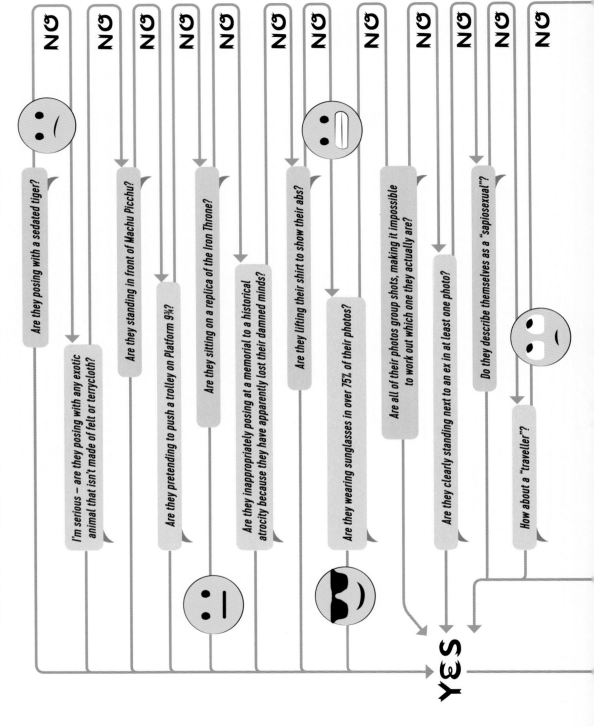

SHOULD YOU SWIPE RIGHT?

Are they posing with a sedated tiger? — NO

I'm serious — are they posing with any exotic animal that isn't made of felt or terrycloth? — NO

Are they standing in front of Machu Picchu? — NO

Are they pretending to push a trolley on Platform 9¾? — NO

Are they sitting on a replica of the Iron Throne? — NO

Are they inappropriately posing at a memorial to a historical atrocity because they have apparently lost their damned minds? — NO

Are they lifting their shirt to show their abs? — NO

Are they wearing sunglasses in over 75% of their photos? — NO

Are all of their photos group shots, making it impossible to work out which one they actually are? — NO

Are they clearly standing next to an ex in at least one photo? — NO

Do they describe themselves as a "sapiosexual"? — NO

How about a "traveller"? — NO

YES

52

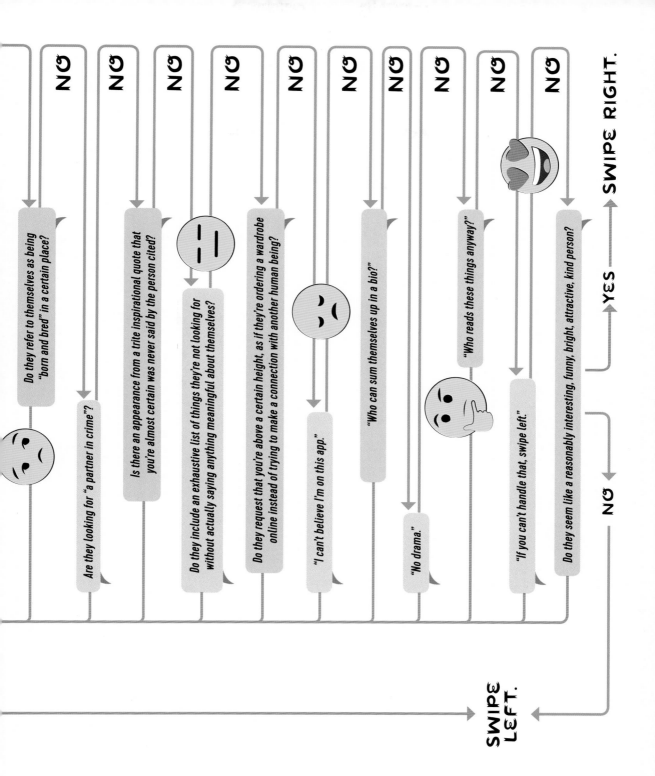

WHY IS THE BOAT SINKING?

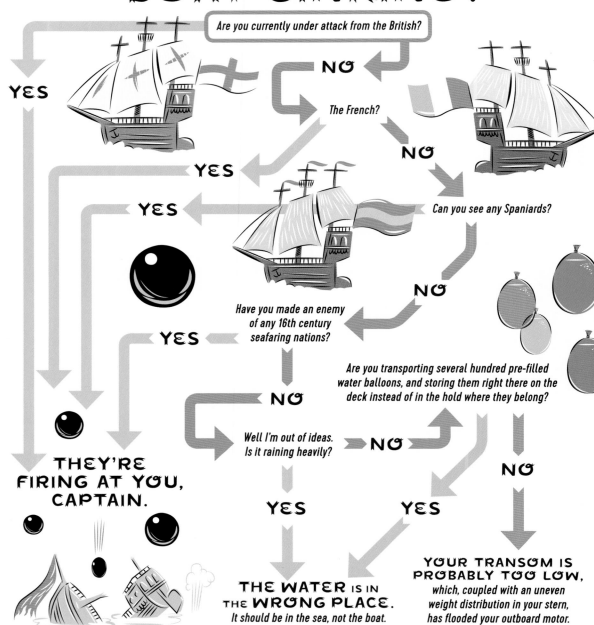

Are you currently under attack from the British?

YES

NO

The French?

YES

NO

YES

Can you see any Spaniards?

NO

Have you made an enemy of any 16th century seafaring nations?

YES

NO

Are you transporting several hundred pre-filled water balloons, and storing them right there on the deck instead of in the hold where they belong?

Well I'm out of ideas. Is it raining heavily?

NO

THEY'RE FIRING AT YOU, CAPTAIN.

YES

YES

NO

THE WATER IS IN THE WRONG PLACE.
It should be in the sea, not the boat.

YOUR TRANSOM IS PROBABLY TOO LOW,
which, coupled with an uneven weight distribution in your stern, has flooded your outboard motor.

ARE YOU CAPABLE OF LASTING EMOTIONAL GROWTH?

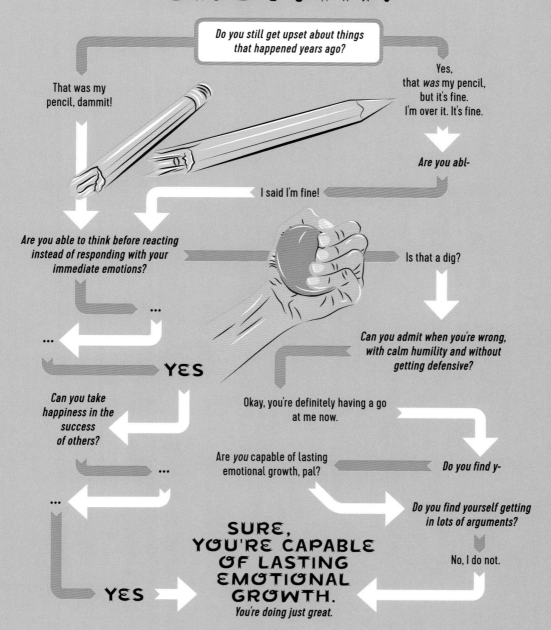

Do you still get upset about things that happened years ago?

That was my pencil, dammit!

Yes, that *was* my pencil, but it's fine. I'm over it. It's fine.

Are you abl-

I said I'm fine!

Are you able to think before reacting instead of responding with your immediate emotions?

...

...

YES

Is that a dig?

Can you admit when you're wrong, with calm humility and without getting defensive?

Can you take happiness in the success of others?

...

Okay, you're definitely having a go at me now.

Are *you* capable of lasting emotional growth, pal?

...

Do you find y-

Do you find yourself getting in lots of arguments?

No, I do not.

SURE, YOU'RE CAPABLE OF LASTING EMOTIONAL GROWTH.

You're doing just great.

YES

SHOULD YOU JOIN MY CULT – WAIT, HA HA HA, DID I SAY CULT?

I MEANT SHOULD YOU JOIN MY GROUP OF LIKE-MINDED PEOPLE THAT LIVE BY A CERTAIN SET OF GUIDELINES WITHIN A COMPOUND AND OF WHOM I JUST SO HAPPEN TO BE THE HONOURABLE ETERNAL LEADER? NOT A CULT.

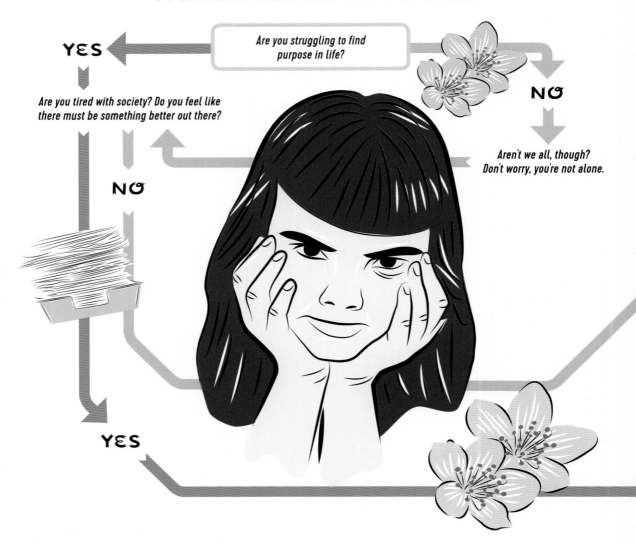

Are you struggling to find purpose in life?

YES

NO

Are you tired with society? Do you feel like there must be something better out there?

Aren't we all, though? Don't worry, you're not alone.

NO

YES

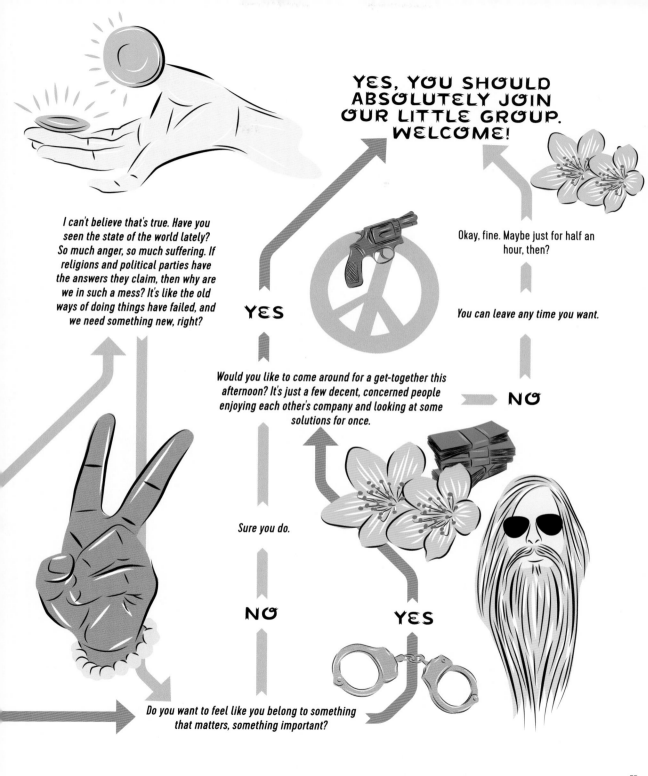

YES, YOU SHOULD ABSOLUTELY JOIN OUR LITTLE GROUP. WELCOME!

I can't believe that's true. Have you seen the state of the world lately? So much anger, so much suffering. If religions and political parties have the answers they claim, then why are we in such a mess? It's like the old ways of doing things have failed, and we need something new, right?

YES

Okay, fine. Maybe just for half an hour, then?

You can leave any time you want.

Would you like to come around for a get-together this afternoon? It's just a few decent, concerned people enjoying each other's company and looking at some solutions for once.

NO

Sure you do.

NO

YES

Do you want to feel like you belong to something that matters, something important?

WHY DID YOUR RELATIONSHIP END?

Did your partner claim to spend hours "at the library" even though you know they can't read?

YES

NO

YES

Did your partner start ghosting you right around the time that a small percentage of the earth's population mysteriously vanished?

Why the relationship ended:
Your growing suspicion that your partner didn't really miss your birthday drinks because of a

"TOP SECRET READING MISSION".

When you used to argue, would your partner refuse to make a genuine effort to listen to your point of view, and also would they mostly just shimmer against the bedroom wall as a car passed by on the street outside?

NO

YES

Why the relationship ended:
Your partner was actually just

THE SHADOW OF A PILE OF CLOTHES ON A CHAIR,
cast against the wall by a street light. You perhaps should have noticed sooner.

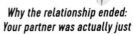

Why the relationship ended:
THEY DISAPPEARED IN THE RAPTURE.

Why the relationship ended:
BASICALLY THE SAME REASON ALL THE OTHER ONES DID.

Why the relationship ended:
YOUR PARTNER HAD A SECRET SECOND FAMILY
who are evidently better than you.

YES

NO

Did you yell at each other all the time, seemingly for no reason?

NO

When you were still together, did you ever spot your partner buying groceries in a supermarket with a group of overly-familiar strangers?

YES

Did your partner invariably pull a face whenever you attended special occasions?

NO

NO

NO

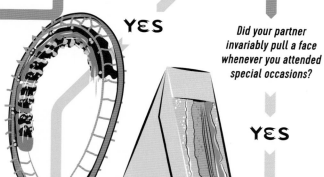

YES

Did your partner die in a tragic speedboat explosion?

YES

Why the relationship ended:
Despite the incredible savings, it was probably
A MISTAKE TO MOVE DIRECTLY BELOW THAT ROLLERCOASTER.

Why the relationship ended:
They were dismayed by your
PERVERSE FONDNESS FOR SANDWICHES WHICH ARE 20 MINUTES TOO OLD
and just starting to atrophy.

Why the relationship ended:
THEY DIED IN A TRAGIC SPEEDBOAT EXPLOSION.

ARE YOU JUST A BRAIN IN A VAT?

Do you feel certain that you are actually experiencing the things you're experiencing?

Wait, what? So if I'm not experiencing the things I'm experiencing then who *is* experiencing the things I'm experiencing? Are *you* experiencing the things you're experiencing?

Look at it this way: the impulses that a brain — your brain, specifically — would receive in a vat are exactly the same as if your brain was right where you think it is, in your own head, at this very moment. So how do you know you're not actually in a vat?

Because I'm not a brain in a vat! I've stubbed my toe on every table I've ever owned. My cheeks tingle when I eat caramel. My right thumb clicks for no reason. I've picked wild blackberries. I've lost snowball fights. I need a new office chair. I'm alive.

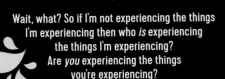

That's exactly what a brain in a vat would say.

Maybe I can close my eyes and try to sloosh myself around?

In that case, what does it matter?

I'm starting to worry you might just be an empty vat, filled with some sort of dimwitted saline solution.

Slooshing

Now we're getting somewhere!

YOU ARE A BRAIN IN A VAT!
Or maybe you're not? Who can say?

Can you just leave me to my life/false-life-inside-a-vat now, please?

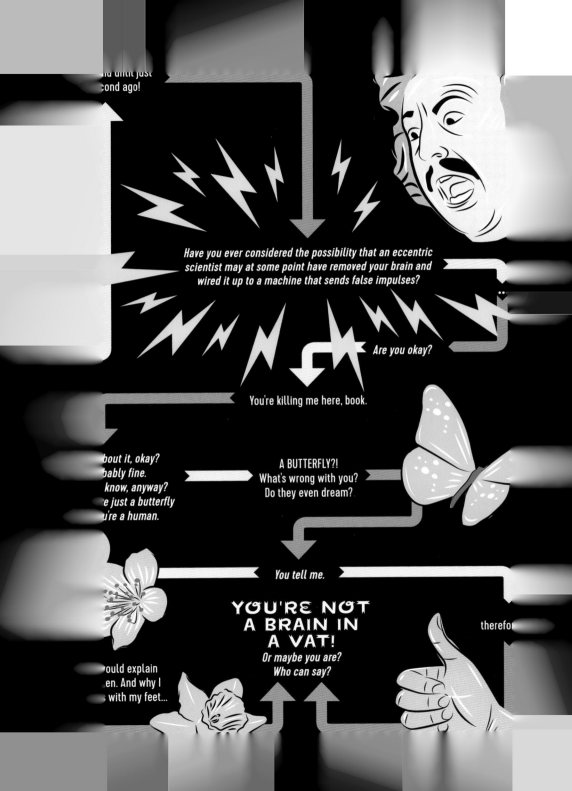

THE SUN HAS EXPLODED AND ALL LIFE ON EARTH WILL END IN EIGHT MINUTES.
WHAT SHOULD YOU DO?

I'm sorry to be the one to break it to you, but society crumbled during this sentence. There's chaos in the streets, fornication left and right, people are looting ice cream vans, the phone reception is like 12:01 on New Year's Eve... you've got eight minutes to live.

And I don't even like New Year's.

EEP!

If someone isn't nearby then you're not getting to them before the end, and who would want to spend their final living moments jogging?

I know it sounds weird, but actually that sounds okay to me.

Um, can you hurry it up *a little*?

You're right, you're right. I'm trying to say that your options are limited. So... are you a fan of nearly-forgotten attempts at solo careers from 90s boyband members?

Great! in that case,
GO FOR A JOG.
No need to stretch first.

YES

NO

LISTEN TO "FOUR MINUTE WARNING"
by Mark Owen, twice!

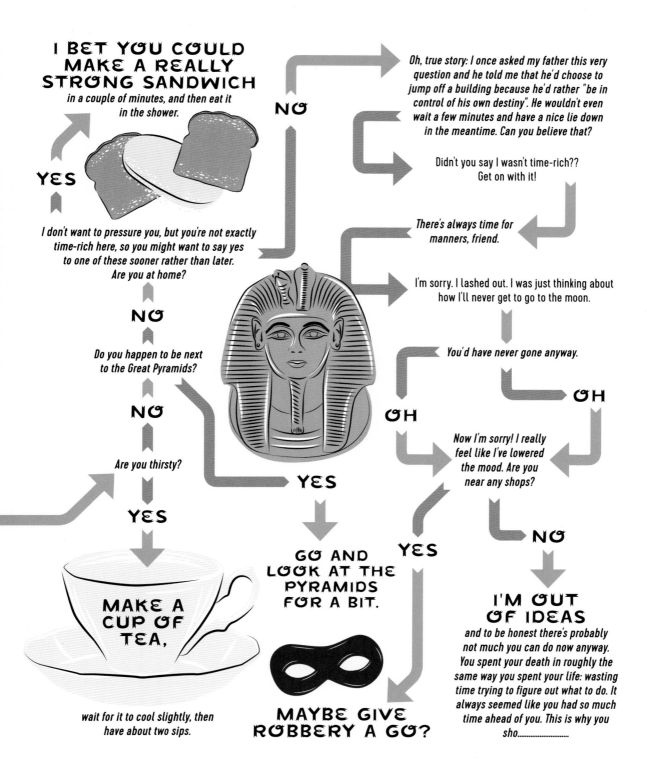

I BET YOU COULD MAKE A REALLY STRONG SANDWICH in a couple of minutes, and then eat it in the shower.

YES

I don't want to pressure you, but you're not exactly time-rich here, so you might want to say yes to one of these sooner rather than later. Are you at home?

NO

Do you happen to be next to the Great Pyramids?

NO

Are you thirsty?

YES

NO

Oh, true story: I once asked my father this very question and he told me that he'd choose to jump off a building because he'd rather "be in control of his own destiny". He wouldn't even wait a few minutes and have a nice lie down in the meantime. Can you believe that?

Didn't you say I wasn't time-rich?? Get on with it!

There's always time for manners, friend.

I'm sorry. I lashed out. I was just thinking about how I'll never get to go to the moon.

You'd have never gone anyway.

OH

OH

Now I'm sorry! I really feel like I've lowered the mood. Are you near any shops?

YES

MAKE A CUP OF TEA,

wait for it to cool slightly, then have about two sips.

YES

GO AND LOOK AT THE PYRAMIDS FOR A BIT.

YES

MAYBE GIVE ROBBERY A GO?

NO

I'M OUT OF IDEAS and to be honest there's probably not much you can do now anyway. You spent your death in roughly the same way you spent your life: wasting time trying to figure out what to do. It always seemed like you had so much time ahead of you. This is why you sho............................

63

WHAT MAKES LIFE WORTH LIVING?

There's nothing bigger than the little things — except, of course, for...

The world's biggest pizza, which I haven't seen but you've got to assume is huge, right?

The popularity of Phil Collins in the mid-80s. I know he looked like a bank manager, but seriously, he sold over 150 million albums.

Pepperoni or roasted vegetables?

"In The Air Tonight" or *"Against All Odds"?*

Pepperoni.

Roasted vegetables.

"In The Air Tonight".

"Against All Odds".

GOING TO A PUB
and finding some empty chairs next to a roaring fire.

When you think one of your plants has died but then it **ROARS BACK TO LIFE**.

When you pour your water from the washing-up bowl into the sink and for a minute the **BOWL FLOATS AROUND LIKE A BOAT.**

THE WARMTH OF A MUG OF TEA
as you hold it in your hands.

My appetite for the bread they serve in restaurants before they bring your meal out, which is apparently bottomless.

One of those cruise ships that are roughly the size of Iceland and look fun but you'd probably have a deep existential crisis about three days in.

Symphony of the Seas or Harmony of the Seas, which the internet tells me are both massive, slightly-depressing cruise ships?

"Bread" or "Don't fill up on bread, you'll ruin your appetite"?

Bread.

Don't fill up on bread, you'll ruin your appetite.

Harmony of the Seas.

Symphony of the Seas.

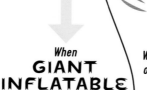

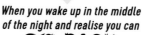

An hour alone in a cafe, just
READING AND BEING WITH YOURSELF.

When
GIANT INFLATABLE ANIMALS
break free of their tethers and tumble down motorways.

When you wake up in the middle of the night and realise you can
GO BACK TO SLEEP
because you don't have to be up for hours.

Using
TWICE THE AMOUNT OF GARLIC
than the recipe specifies.

CHAPTER 4

Work, work, work, work, work, work

THIS IS A RIHANNA REFERENCE AND ALSO AN ACCURATE REPRESENTATION OF WORK. UNLESS YOU'RE RIHANNA, I ASSUME. SHE PROBABLY LOVES HER JOB. HI RIHANNA! THANKS FOR YOUR PURCHASE. TELL YOUR PALS!

SHOULD YOU TAKE A JOB AS A **NIGHTWATCHMAN**
AT THAT CREEPY ABANDONED FAIRGROUND

(WHICH CLOSED DOWN IN MYSTERIOUS CIRCUMSTANCES FOLLOWING A SERIES OF UNSOLVED MURDERS?)

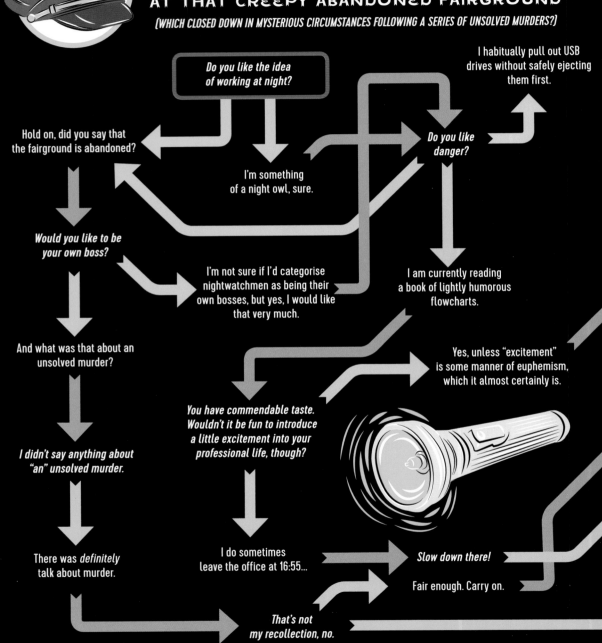

Do you like the idea of working at night?

I habitually pull out USB drives without safely ejecting them first.

Hold on, did you say that the fairground is abandoned?

I'm something of a night owl, sure.

Do you like danger?

Would you like to be your own boss?

I'm not sure if I'd categorise nightwatchmen as being their own bosses, but yes, I would like that very much.

I am currently reading a book of lightly humorous flowcharts.

And what was that about an unsolved murder?

Yes, unless "excitement" is some manner of euphemism, which it almost certainly is.

You have commendable taste. Wouldn't it be fun to introduce a little excitement into your professional life, though?

I didn't say anything about "an" unsolved murder.

There was *definitely* talk about murder.

I do sometimes leave the office at 16:55...

Slow down there!

Fair enough. Carry on.

That's not my recollection, no.

Does my dentist count?

I was lying about having a dentist. I wanted you to think I was cool.

You should absolutely take a job at that

CREEPY ABANDONED FAIRGROUND

(which closed down in mysterious circumstances following a series of unsolved murders). I mean, what's the worst that could happen? Or, at least, what's the twelfth or thirteenth worst thing that could happen? It'll be fine. It'll probably be fine.

Would they be able to recognise your body if, say, there was nothing left of you... except your teeth?

Do you have any loved ones who might notice your sudden disappearance?

A firm yes.

I don't think a career as a nightwatchman is for you. Oh hey,

WHAT'S THAT BEHIND YOU?

Honestly, this isn't a ruse. I'm not about to do something. I'm a book. There's something behind you. Go on, check for yourself. I dare you.

How fast can you run?

Well, I start to shut down my computer and get my coat at 16:55...

Faster than anyone holding a chainsaw, pal.

If I wanted a job that involved running I'd visit the local leisure centre and become a professional athlete. Is that where you sign up for that sort of thing?

I've, uhh, just remembered

WHY DIDN'T THE JOB INTERVIEW GO WELL?

Did you do any preparation in advance?

I researched the company, studied the job description carefully and thought of examples from my own experience to demonstrate why I was a strong candidate.

What did you wear?

Smart clothes that were appropriate for the position.

I told a pre-prepared story about a team failure, identifying what went wrong and how it could have been avoided, demonstrating a capacity for insight, self-reflection and personal responsibility.

What did you say when they asked you to tell them about a time you failed professionally?

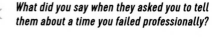

I didn't catch one of their questions and so I politely got them to repeat it.

Any awkward moments?

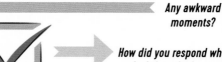

How did you respond when the interviewers asked if you had any questions for them?

I asked them what their favourite thing was about working for the company.

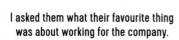

What went wrong:

THEY WERE ALWAYS PLANNING TO HIRE SOMEONE FROM WITHIN

but were legally required to advertise the job externally. Why don't you forget your troubles with a drink?

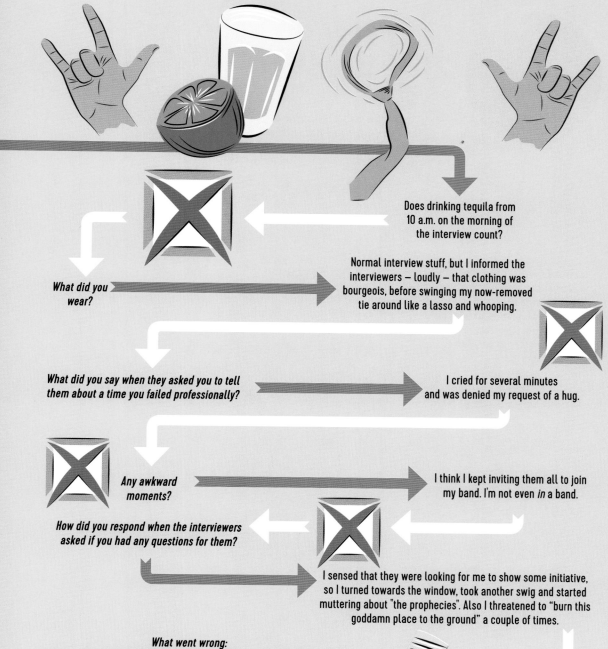

Does drinking tequila from 10 a.m. on the morning of the interview count?

What did you wear?

Normal interview stuff, but I informed the interviewers — loudly — that clothing was bourgeois, before swinging my now-removed tie around like a lasso and whooping.

What did you say when they asked you to tell them about a time you failed professionally?

I cried for several minutes and was denied my request of a hug.

Any awkward moments?

I think I kept inviting them all to join my band. I'm not even *in* a band.

How did you respond when the interviewers asked if you had any questions for them?

I sensed that they were looking for me to show some initiative, so I turned towards the window, took another swig and started muttering about "the prophecies". Also I threatened to "burn this goddamn place to the ground" a couple of times.

What went wrong:
YOU PROBABLY SHOULDN'T HAVE BROUGHT HARD LIQUOR IN WITH YOU,
especially as you refused to share it.

HOW SHOULD YOU REBRAND YOURSELF?

The market research is in: people are growing tired of you.

But I'm not a company?

That's exactly what Craig Slist told me and I exposed him to all sorts of new key demographics. I can do the same for you! What complaint do you hear most about yourself from friends, family, retailers, customers, romantic partners and suppliers?

My name is too easy to pronounce and spell.

I'm not edgy enough and my colours are too vibrant and interesting instead of a sludgy grey-brown.

My shareholders are going to freak out.

How attached are you to actually being "you"?

VERY

NOT VERY

REMOVE ALL OF THE VOWELS FROM YOUR NAME.

JSN WRD
CEO

Spend millions on an ostentatious design agency (hiya!) and just end up putting the word **"NEW"** in front of your name.

YOUNGER AND MORE ATTRACTIVE PERSON
to depict you.

Cast a

A GRITTY REBOOT.

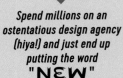

WHERE SHOULD YOU HIDE YOUR STOLEN TREASURE?

YES

Would you like your treasure to become unrecoverable because the environment will inevitably change over the years, eventually rendering your treasure map inaccurate even if no-one rats you out or steals the hoard first?

NO, OBVIOUSLY

BURY IT,
anywhere you like: a canyon, a lonesome atoll, Luton Airport, under a specific kind of tree, under a different specific kind of tree. You just have to put it underground and wait for time to take it — like it takes everything else — away.

In that case you should find a location where no-one ever goes. Is your stolen treasure very thin?

NO

YES

YOU SHOULD HIDE YOUR TREASURE INSIDE A PRINTED NEWSPAPER.

YOU SHOULD HIDE YOUR TREASURE INSIDE A BLOCKBUSTER VIDEO STORE IN 2009.
Burn! Take that, Blockbuster Video and its failure to embrace streaming amid the decline of physical media and become Netflix. You could have had it all!

HOW CAN YOU MAKE YOUR DEADLINE?

Your deadline is approaching, but that's okay: you've got plenty of time left. What should you do now?

Check to see if anyone's e-mailed you in the past ten minutes.

Check to see if anyone has said anything interesting on social media.

Clean your keyboard.

Pop on wikipedia to quickly look up something. Three hours later find yourself with 47 tabs open including "Death by coconut", "Coffee production in Brazil", "Spud (Nickname)", "List of newspapers by circulation", "Jimmy Carter rabbit incident", "Candy (Cameo song)" and "Devil's Beef Tub".

Take a walk for "inspiration".

WORK

Clean your entire home.

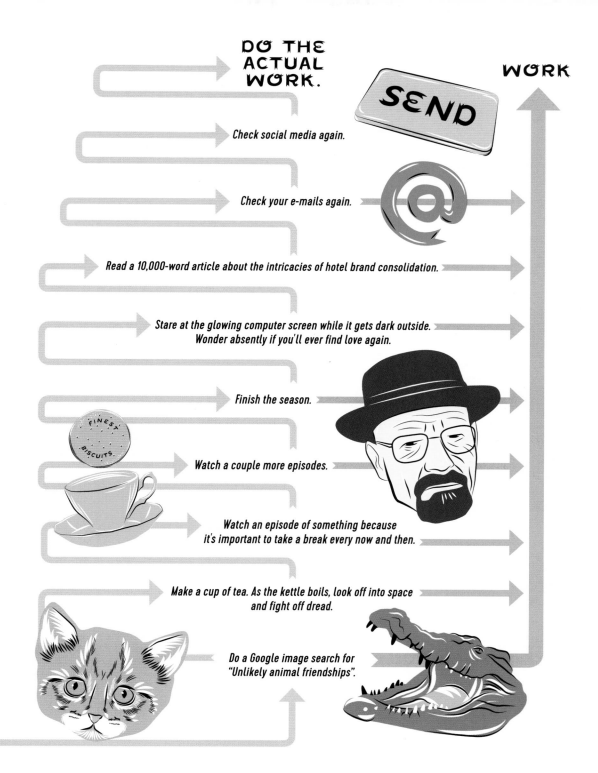

DO THE ACTUAL WORK.

WORK

SEND

Check social media again.

Check your e-mails again.

Read a 10,000-word article about the intricacies of hotel brand consolidation.

Stare at the glowing computer screen while it gets dark outside. Wonder absently if you'll ever find love again.

Finish the season.

FINEST BISCUITS.

Watch a couple more episodes.

Watch an episode of something because it's important to take a break every now and then.

Make a cup of tea. As the kettle boils, look off into space and fight off dread.

Do a Google image search for "Unlikely animal friendships".

SHOULD YOU CONSIDER A LIFE OF CRIME?

Do you have any skills that might aid your nascent criminal career?

I can bring my own balaclava?

I'm a master forger and can crack any safe.

I'm an ace at breaching statutory tort law.

What would you do if the police were closing in on you?

Does the idea of carrying out an audacious bank heist appeal to you?

Not really.

Absolutely — I hate those little pens.

Afraid, are you?

In a stunning third act twist, you'd learn that I'm actually a dirty cop when I dispassionately gun down the protagonist's best friend after they figure out that I've been crooked this whole time.

I'd evade detection by stealing a hat and joining a parade that's conveniently passing by.

MAYBE START BY KNOCKING OFF A MINIATURE GOLF COURSE
and see how that goes?

No, it's just that the chance of being caught is disproportionately high, a third of all bank robberies fail completely and the average haul is usually a few thousand dollars, less than six months at any minimum wage job. The illegal lumber trade, now *that's* where the money is.

YOU SHOULD ABSOLUTELY CONSIDER A LIFE OF CRIME.
You're such a natural, people are going to accuse you of being a cliché!

I'M SORRY,
they don't let spoilsports become criminals.

Did you not hear that I have my own balaclava?

I CAN'T MAKE OUT WHAT YOU'RE SAYING, CAN YOU TAKE THAT THING OFF?

Are you able to be discreet?

NOPE.

I WOULDN'T ADVISE BECOMING A CRIMINAL UNTIL YOU LEARN TO USE YOUR INDOOR VOICE.

Unless you want to work outside, I suppose — from my very secret sources I've been hearing that the illegal lumber trade is blowing up right now.

I definitely won't betray you at some crucial moment for a bigger share of the score.

NOT ONLY SHOULD YOU CONSIDER A LIFE OF CRIME,

I'd be thrilled if you'd join my crew. We're doing one last job and then I'm flying the coop with my lover. Are you in?

It's weird that you would bring that up unprompted, but okay.

Look, I'm saying that I'm *not* going shoot you in the back as soon we've finished the job and then skip the country with your lover and two gym bags filled with non-sequential bank notes.

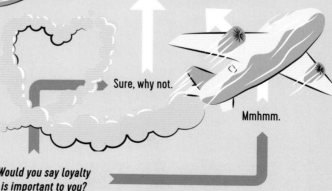

Sure, why not.

Mmhmm.

Would you say loyalty is important to you?

WILL YOU MAKE IT IN THE
MUSIC INDUSTRY?

Are you willing the accept the notion that although talent, dedication, originality, ambition and discipline are enormously important, your musical future is also just as likely to depend on a bunch of random, intangible factors beyond your control?

NO

YES

Describe your hairstyle.

Um, well it's definitely not a mop head that got stuck to my scalp several years ago and I forgot to get it removed. On a totally separate point, a friend of mine wondered if you have any advice on how to remove a bundle of slighty damp yarn that's been attached to their skin for some time now?

12 minutes ahead of its time.

Business in the front, party in the back, business-casual in the middle.

YOU WILL MAKE IT IN THE MUSIC INDUSTRY,
but every now and then you'll ask yourself if it was all worth it. Yes, yes it was.

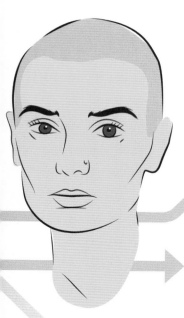

"A bold choice".

YOU WON'T MAKE IT IN THE MUSIC INDUSTRY,

but at least you'll never have to do an endless residency in Las Vegas that brings you hundreds of millions of dollars and virtually no joy.

Probably not.

I'm not quite sure how to describe my hair but a family of chaffinches recently made their home in it, does that help? They seem friendly.

Are you any good at coming up with rhymes for the word "Baby"?

Maybe I am...

SORT OF.

While you'll never escape the gravitational pull of your one-hit wonder, that hit will allow you to travel the world (albeit the parts that include county fairs) playing music for a career, which was all you really wanted to do with your life anyway. Your entire artistic output will be defined by some dumb confection you wrote in an afternoon, but those three impossibly-catchy minutes will make people laugh and cry and dance at wedding discos — forever.

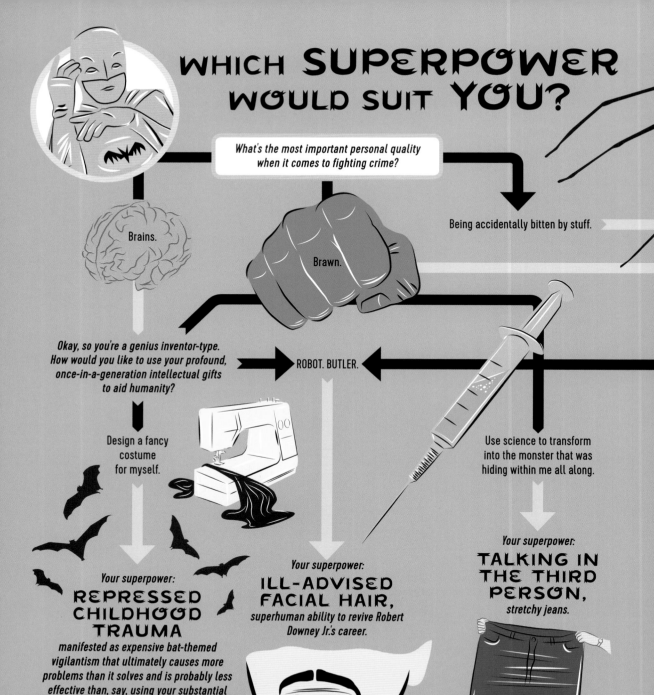

WHICH SUPERPOWER WOULD SUIT YOU?

What's the most important personal quality when it comes to fighting crime?

Brains.

Brawn.

Being accidentally bitten by stuff.

Okay, so you're a genius inventor-type. How would you like to use your profound, once-in-a-generation intellectual gifts to aid humanity?

ROBOT. BUTLER.

Design a fancy costume for myself.

Use science to transform into the monster that was hiding within me all along.

Your superpower:
TALKING IN THE THIRD PERSON,
stretchy jeans.

Your superpower:
REPRESSED CHILDHOOD TRAUMA
manifested as expensive bat-themed vigilantism that ultimately causes more problems than it solves and is probably less effective than, say, using your substantial fortune to fund city-wide infrastructure projects and public health initiatives.

Your superpower:
ILL-ADVISED FACIAL HAIR,
superhuman ability to revive Robert Downey Jr.'s career.

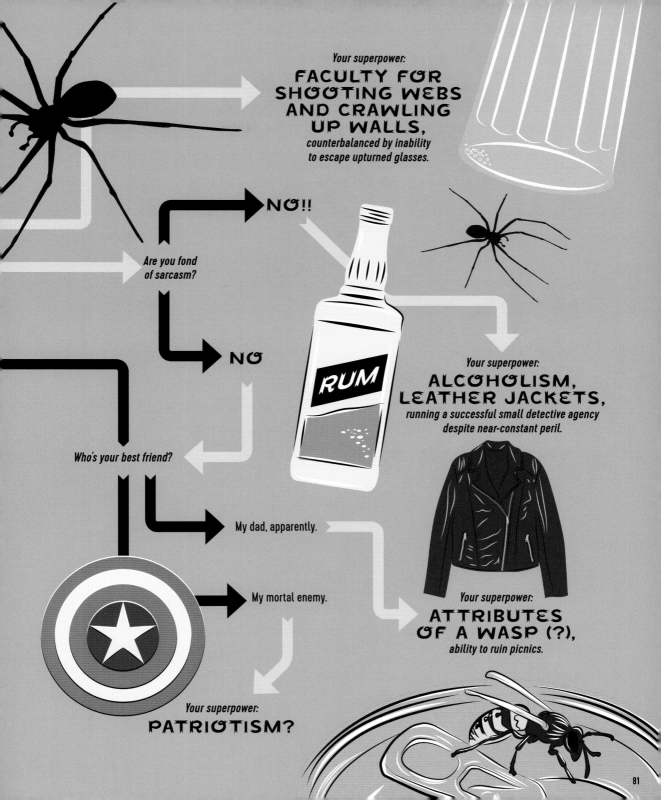

Your superpower:
FACULTY FOR SHOOTING WEBS AND CRAWLING UP WALLS,
counterbalanced by inability to escape upturned glasses.

NO!!

Are you fond of sarcasm?

NO

Who's your best friend?

My dad, apparently.

My mortal enemy.

Your superpower:
ALCOHOLISM, LEATHER JACKETS,
running a successful small detective agency despite near-constant peril.

Your superpower:
ATTRIBUTES OF A WASP (?),
ability to ruin picnics.

Your superpower:
PATRIOTISM?

RUM

SHOULD YOU FINALLY GET AROUND TO FIXING
THAT DRAWER THAT'S BEEN BOTHERING YOU FOR AGES?

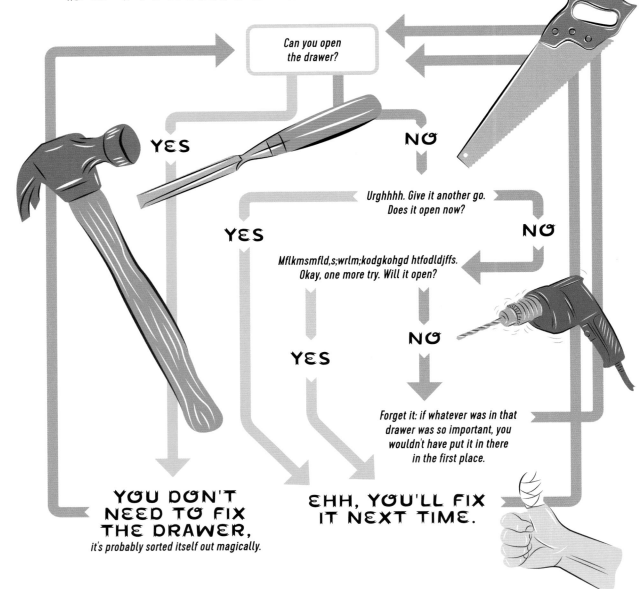

Can you open the drawer?

YES

NO

Urghhhh. Give it another go. Does it open now?

YES

NO

Mflkmsmfld,s;wrlm;kodgkohgd htfodldjffs. Okay, one more try. Will it open?

YES

NO

Forget it: if whatever was in that drawer was so important, you wouldn't have put it in there in the first place.

YOU DON'T NEED TO FIX THE DRAWER,
it's probably sorted itself out magically.

EHH, YOU'LL FIX IT NEXT TIME.

WHAT SHOULD BE YOUR NEW CAREER?

You took a long, long walk, that weekend you were made redundant. It was disappointing to lose your job, you reflected, but maybe it was an oppportunity too. How good would it feel to finally leave office-work behind and try something new!

You've resolved to be flexible about whatever comes next, which is fortunate considering that the only jobs available are in the 19th century, and the commute will be a nightmare.

Your new career:
Middle management in a
GANG OF CHILD PICKPOCKETS.

Your new career:
A prospector
FRUITLESSLY PANNING FOR GOLD
during a gold rush and dying penniless — you do get a nice hat out of it, though.

Dodging things (artfully).

So let's narrow things down a bit: do you have any hobbies?

Sitting in a river (unsuccessfully).

Watching movies on television, playing video games, using a smartphone to communicate with people on other continents via the internet, eating cornflakes, using crayons and hair dryers and teabags, being aware that the dwarf planet Pluto exists, not dying of smallpox...

Oh crumbs. Do you also happen to enjoy ducking under a bar when impromptu gunfights break out?

NO

How would you describe your feelings towards whales?

YES

BANG

CORN FLAKES

Monomaniacal self-defeating hatred.

Neutral.

Your new career:
Put-upon
SALOON OWNER.

Your new career:
CAPTAIN OF A NANTUCKET WHALING SHIP,
prosthetic limb enthusiast.

Alright, then it's
OFF TO THE WORKHOUSE
with you, I'm afraid.

CHAPTER 5

Hobbies! Art! Movies! Literature! Videogames! Music! Punctuation!

SHOULD'VE COME UP WITH A SNAPPIER NAME FOR THIS ONE, REALLY

WHICH 90S FAD ARE YOU?

Ah, the 1990s.
As the song goes:
Smells like...

Teen spirit.

Pogs?
Am I getting
this right?

*They called it the
ship of dreams...*

*Pogs were brightly-coloured
discs that children,
gathered together on
pavements, would try to win
from each other.*

And it was.
It really, really was.

Did they, though? I understand that
Titanic deliberately paints with broad
strokes — a key reason for its global
success and enduring resonance —
but I struggle to believe that someone
in 1912 wou-

Are you sure that wasn't
a fad in the 1940s?

*Let's try another.
Getting jiggy...*

*No, you're thinking
of Polio.*

Wit it.

Getting "jiggy"? People really
had nothing to worry about
back then, did they?

Fun fact: polio was originally played
with bottle caps from a juice
that contained passion fruit,
orange and guava, hence the name.

How else am I going to pay
off my student loans?

You're a
TAMAGOTCHI.

You're an
EXTENDED PERIOD
OF RELATIVE GLOBAL
PROSPERITY AND PEACE
that would seem in retrospect like a kind of idyll.

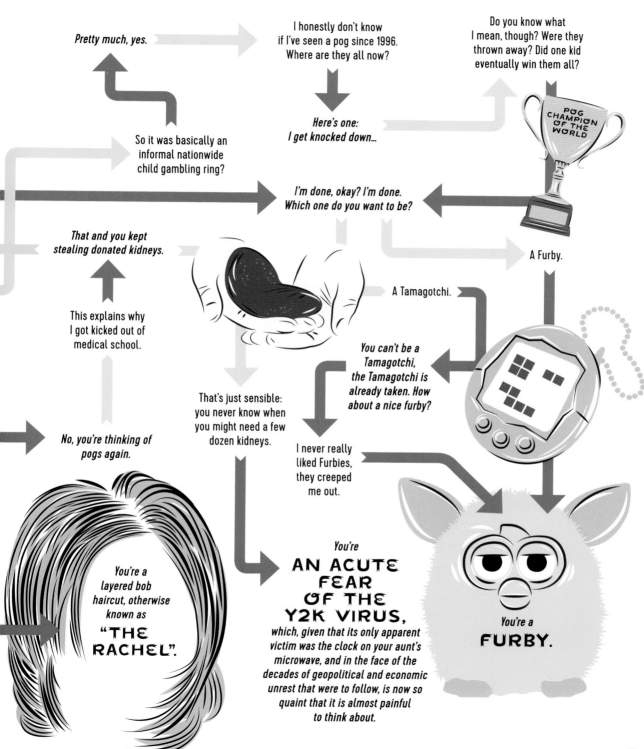

Pretty much, yes.

I honestly don't know if I've seen a pog since 1996. Where are they all now?

Do you know what I mean, though? Were they thrown away? Did one kid eventually win them all?

So it was basically an informal nationwide child gambling ring?

Here's one: I get knocked down...

POG CHAMPION OF THE WORLD

That and you kept stealing donated kidneys.

I'm done, okay? I'm done. Which one do you want to be?

A Furby.

A Tamagotchi.

This explains why I got kicked out of medical school.

You can't be a Tamagotchi, the Tamagotchi is already taken. How about a nice furby?

No, you're thinking of pogs again.

That's just sensible: you never know when you might need a few dozen kidneys.

I never really liked Furbies, they creeped me out.

You're a layered bob haircut, otherwise known as "THE RACHEL".

You're AN ACUTE FEAR OF THE Y2K VIRUS, which, given that its only apparent victim was the clock on your aunt's microwave, and in the face of the decades of geopolitical and economic unrest that were to follow, is now so quaint that it is almost painful to think about.

You're a FURBY.

ARE YOU LIVING IN A MUSICAL?

What typically happens when you walk down the street?

The townsfolk — apparently my neighbourhood has a lot of townsfolk — talk among themselves merrily before breaking into an elaborate production number.

I haven't noticed anything especially noteworthy, but then it's hard to think about much except this loquacious killer plant I've been looking after.

Hugh Jackman keeps singing at me.

How about when you reach your destination?

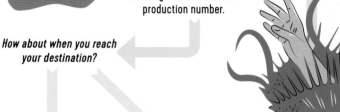

YOU'RE NOT LIVING IN A MUSICAL I'M AFRAID.
Hugh Jackman just loves to sing.

If I'm unsatisfied with my status quo, I'll usually sing a song explaining my primary desire (what "I want", if you'd like), and will probably end up reprising this later unless I have dinner plans.

Not much until a cathartic moment of show stopping revelation, usually around 11 o'clock in the evening.

Is it wise to have that as a pet/houseplant?

My loquacious killer plant is harmless! Here's a wacky idea: do you want to come around and see it?

YOU'RE LIVING IN A MUSICAL.
Watch out for obsessive police inspectors/shot-putting headmistresses/child gangsters/the Jets/ the Nazis/the difficulty in making a relationship work when you both have contrasting ambitions in acting and jazz respectively/duels with Aaron Burr/ gentrification in early 90s Lower Manhattan/demon barbers of Fleet Street/Andrew Lloyd Webber.

YOU'RE LIVING IN A MUSICAL.
And I have... an appointment that I need to get to.

HOW SHOULD YOU ASK A STRANGER FOR DIRECTIONS IN A FOREIGN COUNTRY?

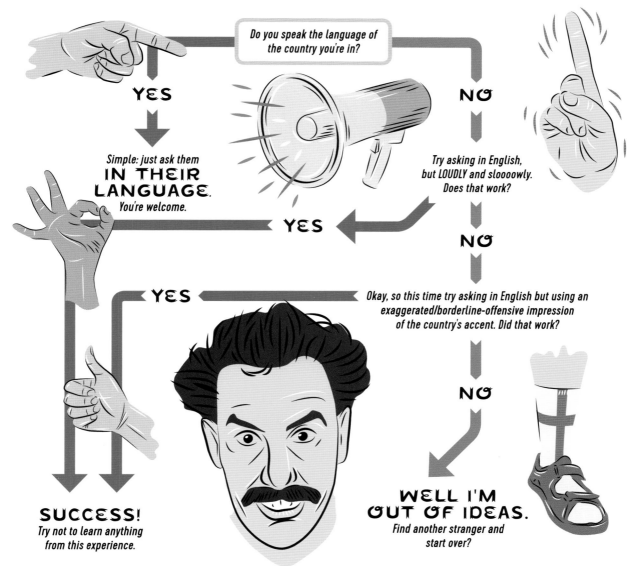

Do you speak the language of the country you're in?

YES

Simple: just ask them **IN THEIR LANGUAGE.** You're welcome.

NO

Try asking in English, but LOUDLY and slooooowly. Does that work?

YES

NO

YES

Okay, so this time try asking in English but using an exaggerated/borderline-offensive impression of the country's accent. Did that work?

NO

SUCCESS!
Try not to learn anything from this experience.

WELL I'M OUT OF IDEAS.
Find another stranger and start over?

WHICH INFAMOUS WORK OF ART ARE YOU?

NO

Do you ever wake up feeling like an assembly of everyday objects, as if you were created as a violent rejection of logic in the wake of a global conflict?

YES

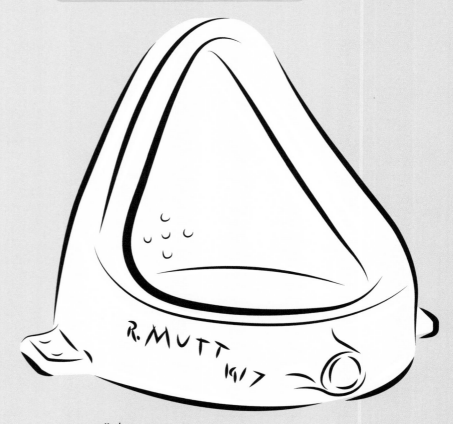

You're

FOUNTAIN
BY MARCEL DUCHAMP.

It's never an easy day when you have to tell someone that they're an upturned urinal, but here we are.

Do you ever feel like a confessional self-portrait expressed through the wayward (although slightly too deliberate?) arrangement of one's most intimate possessions, but you're also, like, an unmade bed that's somehow going to make everyone incredibly angry even though no-one's forcing them to look at it?

YES

You're

MY BED
BY TRACEY EMIN.

The art critic Adrian Seale once called you a self-regarding bore and sometime after that a couple of Japanese performance artists held a pillow fight on top of you, so it's been an eventful life at least.

NO

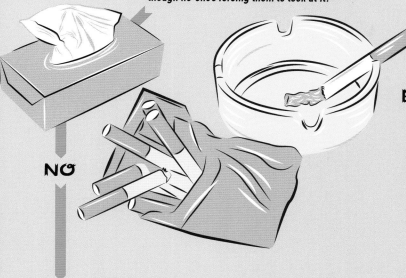

Um, do you ever feel like a group of dogs playing poker? No reason, I'm just curious.

You're

A FRIEND IN NEED
BY CASSIUS MARCELLUS COOLIDGE.

Yes, yes, we're all stunned, you're that painting of dogs playing poker, astonishing scenes. Now that I have you here, I just want to talk real quick about CM Coolidge.

According to his delirious Wikipedia entry, between 1868 and 1872, Coolidge "worked as a druggist and sign painter, founded a bank and a newspaper, then moved from Antwerp, New York, to Rochester, where he started painting dogs in human situations." What was going on with the job market in the 19th century?

NO

YES

Sorry, I know they were rum options, but now you're all out of them. It's time to face hard facts:

MAYBE YOU'RE NOT AN INFAMOUS WORK OF ART AFTER ALL.

AT LONG LAST, HOW WILL YOU MASTER THE GAME "HIDE & SEEK"?

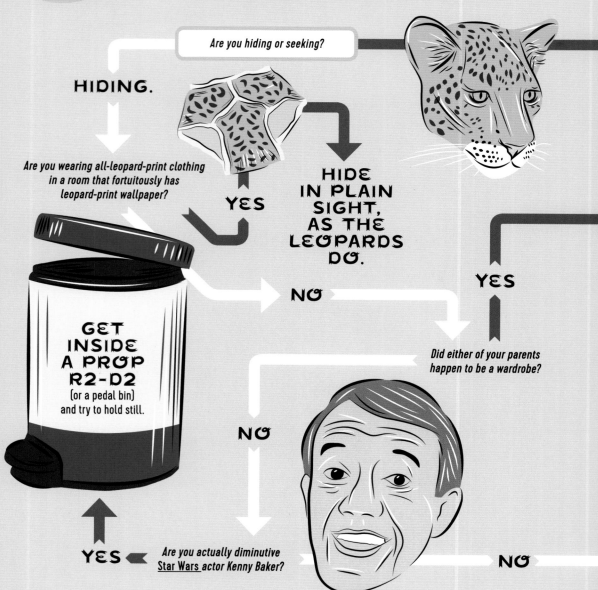

Are you hiding or seeking?

HIDING.

Are you wearing all-leopard-print clothing in a room that fortuitously has leopard-print wallpaper?

YES

HIDE IN PLAIN SIGHT, AS THE LEOPARDS DO.

YES

NO

Did either of your parents happen to be a wardrobe?

GET INSIDE A PROP R2-D2 (or a pedal bin) and try to hold still.

NO

YES

Are you actually diminutive Star Wars actor Kenny Baker?

NO

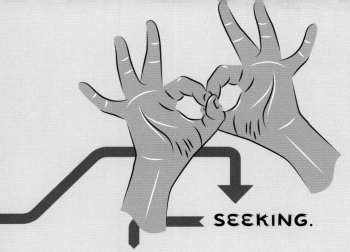

SEEKING.

LOOK UP:
the person you're seeking has somehow gotten the ridiculous idea into their head that high up is the best place to hide. Try ladders and trees.

Is your opponent under the age of 6?

NO

DUDE,
they're just going to be standing somewhere with their hands over their eyes, giggling.

YES

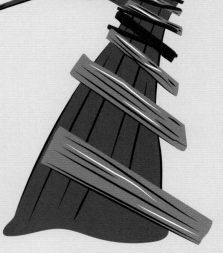

USE YOUR NATURAL WARDROBE -NESS
to blend in with the furniture.

Don't bother climbing under a bed, standing behind a curtain or squeezing into a cupboard –

LOOK FOR A LADDER OR TREE
and try to get as high above the ground as possible. Seriously, give it a go: people don't look up.

WHICH BEATLE ARE YOU?

I am he as you are he as you are me…

What?

And we are all together.

I read the news today, oh boy…

About a worrying decline in governmental accountability and transparency.

About an otter that inadvertently robbed a bank but now looks adorable in a little prison jumpsuit.

About a lucky man who made the grade.

It was twenty years ago today…

All you need is love…

The late 1990s? Didn't I already do the flow chart about that? It turned out I was a Tamagotchi all along. Who knew?

Sgt. Pepper taught the band to play.

Love is all you need.

But I'd also like to have a 120-room mansion in Henley-on-Thames some day.

You're
PAUL McCARTNEY.

Ambitious, organised and always wanting to create the best impression, you are legally obliged to play "Hey Jude" every time you go out in public.

This is why your pets keep dying.

You're
JOHN LENNON.

An irreverent non-conformist and natural leader, you found a look that worked for you and stuck to it.

You're
PETE BEST.

Out of the loop and dispatched early: I'm not going to lie to you, this is the single most depressing answer to receive in the entire book.

Actually my monkey has always been an open book.

Tell me why you cried, and why you lied to me...

Everybody's got something to hide...

Alcohol, and alcohol.

a.) The end of *Babe* when Babe looks up at the farmer, who then nods stoically and says "That'll do pig, that'll do."

b.) Because I didn't want you to know that I was the one who lost your jumper.

Except for me and my monkey.

Why don't we do it in the road?

Will you still need me, will you still feed me, when I'm sixty-four?

Because that's where the cars drive!

I just want to point out that the only other line in this song is "No-one will be watching us", which is almost definitely not true if you're planning on doing it in the road.

Probably not.

You're
RINGO STARR.

Did you know that Ringo was called that because he wore lots of rings? The author of this book only just worked that out and he's been listening to The Beatles for <u>decades</u>. Also, did you know that "The Beatles" is a pun? That's totally not how you spell beetle.

You're
GEORGE HARRISON.

Spiritual, searching and tax-averse, you are often overshadowed by those closest to you, which may explain your fondness for double-denim.

HOW SHOULD YOU FIX YOUR VIDEOGAME CARTRIDGE FROM THE EARLY 90s?

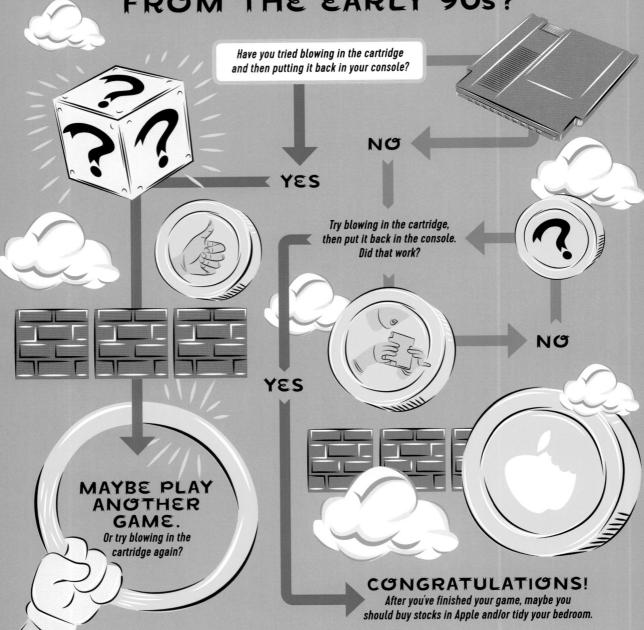

Have you tried blowing in the cartridge and then putting it back in your console?

YES

NO

Try blowing in the cartridge, then put it back in the console. Did that work?

YES

NO

MAYBE PLAY ANOTHER GAME.
Or try blowing in the cartridge again?

CONGRATULATIONS!
After you've finished your game, maybe you should buy stocks in Apple and/or tidy your bedroom.

WHICH LITERARY HERO ARE YOU?

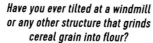
Have you ever tilted at a windmill or any other structure that grinds cereal grain into flour?

NO

YES

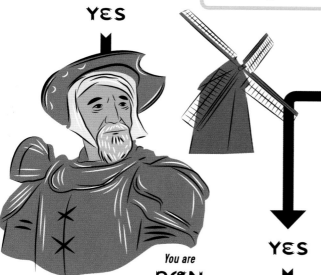

Have you ever lived Eight and Twenty Years, all alone in an un-inhabited Island on the Coast of America, near the Mouth of the Great River of Oroonoque; Having been cast on Shore by Shipwreck, wherein all the Men perished but yourself?

NO

YES

You are
DON QUIXOTE,
Man of La Mancha!

YOU'RE OUT OF OPTIONS, SORRY.
I probably should have mentioned that this flow chart takes place in late October 1721, three months before the publication of Moll Flanders. Hey, I hope the recent deaths of Russian merchants during the sacking of Shamakhi doesn't lead to a Russo-Persian War. And did you hear that the Dutch playwright Abraham Alewijn has died??

You are
ROBINSON CRUSOE,
the slave-trafficking castaway later to become an emblem of cruel British colonialism. Oh dear.

WHICH PUNCTUATION MARK ARE YOU?

What does a panda do?

Eats shoots and leaves.

Refuses to mate.

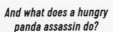

Only eats bamboo despite it having nearly no nutritional value, later tries to garrote an owl.

And what does a hungry panda assassin do?

Eats, shoots and leaves.

It's the bedrock of articulation, and articulation is emancipation.

I see you appreciate good punctuation.

What a thoughtful response.

I don't appreciate your assumptions.

I have more thoughts on the social value of punctuation if you'd like to hear them?

You're a
FULL STOP.

Terse. Reliable. Perfectly round. Maybe you're not as interesting as your peers, but what's a sentence without you? Except for that previous one, obviously.

You're an
ASTERISK

It's a fitting coincidence that the asterisk looks like a star, as that's what you are to conversations: the saviour of a thousand dull exchanges. If matters get too heavy you're usually on hand with some fact about Chrysippus or the etymology of the word "penguin" to defuse the situation. Actually, maybe that's a bit annoying, come to think of it.

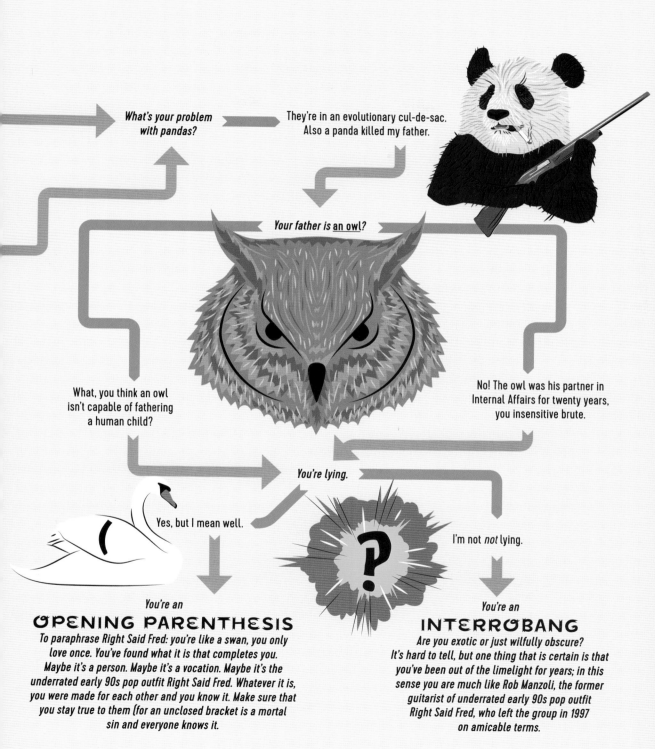

What's your problem with pandas?

They're in an evolutionary cul-de-sac. Also a panda killed my father.

Your father is <u>an owl</u>?

What, you think an owl isn't capable of fathering a human child?

No! The owl was his partner in Internal Affairs for twenty years, you insensitive brute.

You're lying.

Yes, but I mean well.

I'm not *not* lying.

You're an
OPENING PARENTHESIS
To paraphrase Right Said Fred: you're like a swan, you only love once. You've found what it is that completes you. Maybe it's a person. Maybe it's a vocation. Maybe it's the underrated early 90s pop outfit Right Said Fred. Whatever it is, you were made for each other and you know it. Make sure that you stay true to them (for an unclosed bracket is a mortal sin and everyone knows it.

You're an
INTERROBANG
Are you exotic or just wilfully obscure? It's hard to tell, but one thing that is certain is that you've been out of the limelight for years; in this sense you are much like Rob Manzoli, the former guitarist of underrated early 90s pop outfit Right Said Fred, who left the group in 1997 on amicable terms.

WHAT'S MISSING FROM YOUR SCREENPLAY?

Are you ready to figure this out?

"I was born ready."

"I didn't sign up for this!"

Hangs up phone without saying goodbye.

What personal qualities have you given your main character to bring them to life?

What are the key relationships in the movie? How do they evolve?

"Are you trying to get us all killed?"

How about this: what challenges will your protagonist face? How will this affect their outlook and therefore transform their initial motivating desires?

"Secure the perimeter!"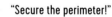

"There's no time to explain!"

I'm sorry, I thought you were looking for my help?

"We've got company."

"That went well."

"Shut up and kiss me."

A POST -COITAL CONVERSATION
under L-shaped bedsheets.

A SCENE IN A MOTEL ROOM
where tweezers are used to remove a bullet from someone's shoulder, after which the spent ammo pings into a metal tray.

A scene where a middle-aged scientist is passed a clipboard by their younger assistant which they read with mounting horror before muttering,
"OH MY GOD".

YE OLDE LOW FAT MEAD

A FUNERAL IN THE RAIN.

Bonus points if the audience is led to believe it's for one character but then it turns out to actually be for another one.

"In English, please."

A GYM-SCULPTED BODY IN A HISTORICAL PERIOD

where food was scarce and nutrition science didn't exist.

"You should have killed me when you had the chance!"

"You just don't get it, do you?"

HENCHMEN WITH BAD AIM.

"I'm in."

A villain whose extraordinarily-risky-in-retrospect plan depends upon

BEING CAPTURED BY THE HERO.

A VILLAIN WITHOUT ANY APPARENT TIME PRESSURES.

A VILLAIN WITH A MONEY-MAKING SCHEME

so convoluted that it's significantly more unreliable and difficult than any actual legal means.

WHICH **BOARD GAME**
ARE YOU?

It's eight o'clock on a Saturday night. Do you want to play a board game?

Do not pass Go. Do not collect £200.

You have won second prize in a beauty contest.

At risk of indigestion

Splendid. The Hungry Hungry Hippos are:

Not going to find happiness in eating.

Complete the following sentence. Siam is...

...an incredibly outdated way to describe Thailand.

...invaluable if you want to protect Australasia in Risk.

 What pawn do you choose in Monopoly?

The racecar.

The dog, placed inside the hat.

Why?

It's a palindrome.

Someone else chose the dog.

YOU'RE CLUEDO.

You smell like a Bakelite telephone and if you had a moustache you would definitely wax it. To you, social status means little: you pal around with colonels and servile chefs, but you distrust them all equally. The downside of this is your vivid sense of paranoia. Danger follows you around so you never let anyone in. Ultimately, you know there's little keeping people from making a bad decision in a Study. Or in a Ballroom. Or in a Kitchen.

YOU'RE MONOPOLY.

You like to travel around London, buying property, dressed as an iron. At your disposal are exceptional negotiating skills that have helped you buy Old Kent Road for £50, which is less than my shoes cost. You also go on for absolutely ages, presumably because you come from a time when people didn't have anything else to do but play Monopoly forever and ever until their eyes bled.

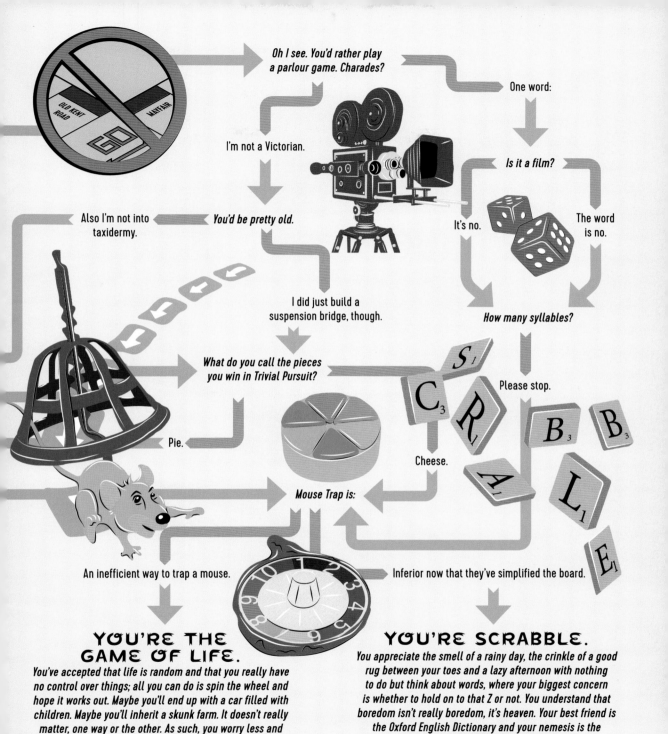

Oh I see. You'd rather play a parlour game. Charades?

One word:

I'm not a Victorian.

Is it a film?

Also I'm not into taxidermy.

You'd be pretty old.

It's no.

The word is no.

I did just build a suspension bridge, though.

How many syllables?

What do you call the pieces you win in Trivial Pursuit?

Please stop.

Pie.

Cheese.

Mouse Trap is:

An inefficient way to trap a mouse.

Inferior now that they've simplified the board.

YOU'RE THE GAME OF LIFE.

You've accepted that life is random and that you really have no control over things; all you can do is spin the wheel and hope it works out. Maybe you'll end up with a car filled with children. Maybe you'll inherit a skunk farm. It doesn't really matter, one way or the other. As such, you worry less and enjoy life more. Also, you think that a racehorse is worth roughly the same as an oil well.

YOU'RE SCRABBLE.

You appreciate the smell of a rainy day, the crinkle of a good rug between your toes and a lazy afternoon with nothing to do but think about words, where your biggest concern is whether to hold on to that Z or not. You understand that boredom isn't really boredom, it's heaven. Your best friend is the Oxford English Dictionary and your nemesis is the 21st century. Good luck to you, friend.

CHAPTER 6

The future

OH BOY

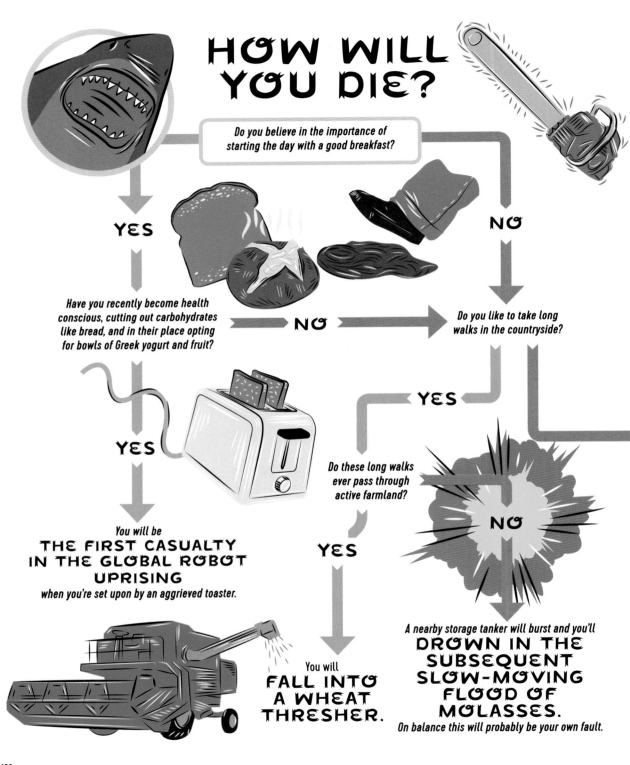

HOW WILL YOU DIE?

Do you believe in the importance of starting the day with a good breakfast?

YES

NO

Have you recently become health conscious, cutting out carbohydrates like bread, and in their place opting for bowls of Greek yogurt and fruit?

NO

Do you like to take long walks in the countryside?

YES

YES

Do these long walks ever pass through active farmland?

NO

You will be
THE FIRST CASUALTY IN THE GLOBAL ROBOT UPRISING
when you're set upon by an aggrieved toaster.

YES

You will
FALL INTO A WHEAT THRESHER.

A nearby storage tanker will burst and you'll
DROWN IN THE SUBSEQUENT SLOW-MOVING FLOOD OF MOLASSES.
On balance this will probably be your own fault.

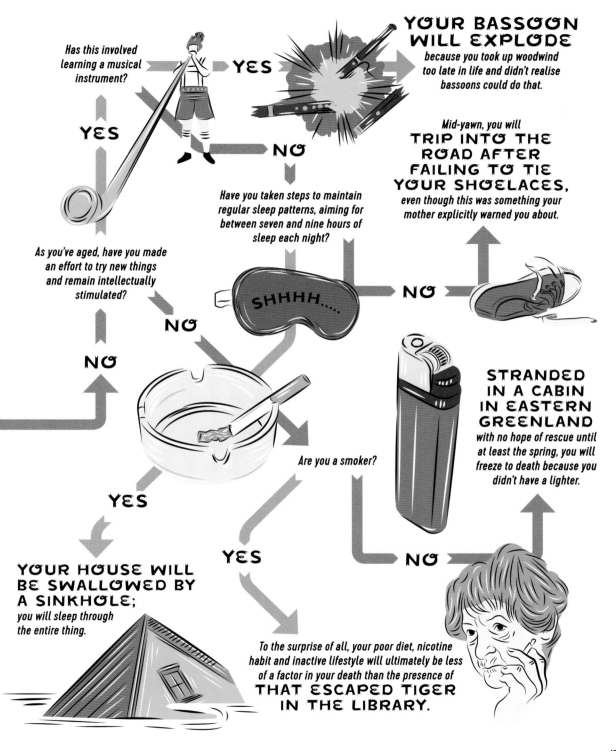

Has this involved learning a musical instrument?

YES → **YOUR BASSOON WILL EXPLODE** because you took up woodwind too late in life and didn't realise bassoons could do that.

YES

As you've aged, have you made an effort to try new things and remain intellectually stimulated?

NO

NO

Have you taken steps to maintain regular sleep patterns, aiming for between seven and nine hours of sleep each night?

NO

Mid-yawn, you will **TRIP INTO THE ROAD AFTER FAILING TO TIE YOUR SHOELACES,** even though this was something your mother explicitly warned you about.

NO

SHHHH.....

NO

Are you a smoker?

STRANDED IN A CABIN IN EASTERN GREENLAND with no hope of rescue until at least the spring, you will freeze to death because you didn't have a lighter.

YES

YES

NO

YOUR HOUSE WILL BE SWALLOWED BY A SINKHOLE; you will sleep through the entire thing.

To the surprise of all, your poor diet, nicotine habit and inactive lifestyle will ultimately be less of a factor in your death than the presence of **THAT ESCAPED TIGER IN THE LIBRARY.**

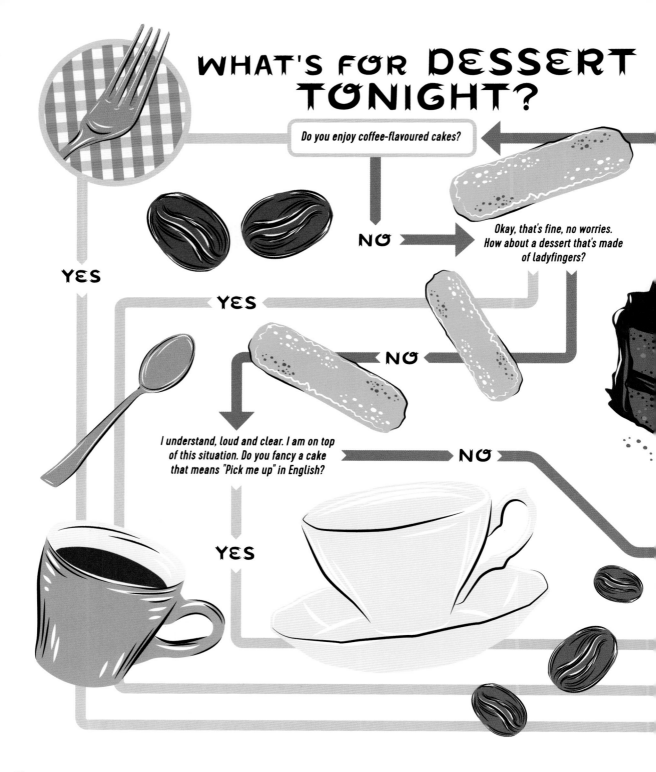

WHAT'S FOR DESSERT TONIGHT?

Do you enjoy coffee-flavoured cakes?

NO

Okay, that's fine, no worries. How about a dessert that's made of ladyfingers?

YES

YES

NO

I understand, loud and clear. I am on top of this situation. Do you fancy a cake that means "Pick me up" in English?

NO

YES

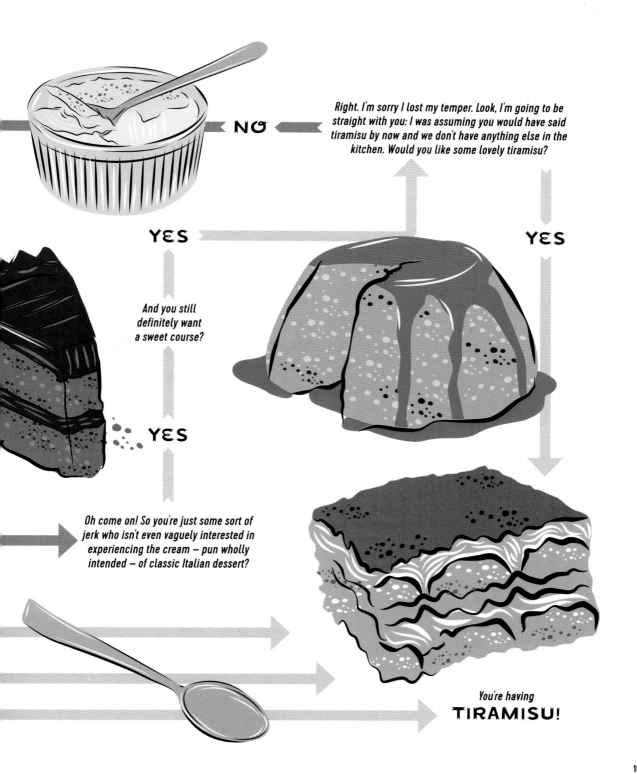

NO

Right. I'm sorry I lost my temper. Look, I'm going to be straight with you: I was assuming you would have said tiramisu by now and we don't have anything else in the kitchen. Would you like some lovely tiramisu?

YES

YES

And you still definitely want a sweet course?

YES

Oh come on! So you're just some sort of jerk who isn't even vaguely interested in experiencing the cream — pun wholly intended — of classic Italian dessert?

You're having

TIRAMISU!

RE WE ALONE IN THE UNIVERSE?

Has security tightened up lately at your local military black site?

→ NO

Have you spotted any unusual lights in the sky?

YES

NO

YES

Do any of your friends have wet, black eyes and suspiciously smooth features?

NO

YES

. That's alarming but e probably just working w reconnaissance aircraft detaining unlawful combatants.

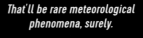

That'll be rare meteorological phenomena, surely.

You've been hanging around with those seals at the aquarium again, haven't you.

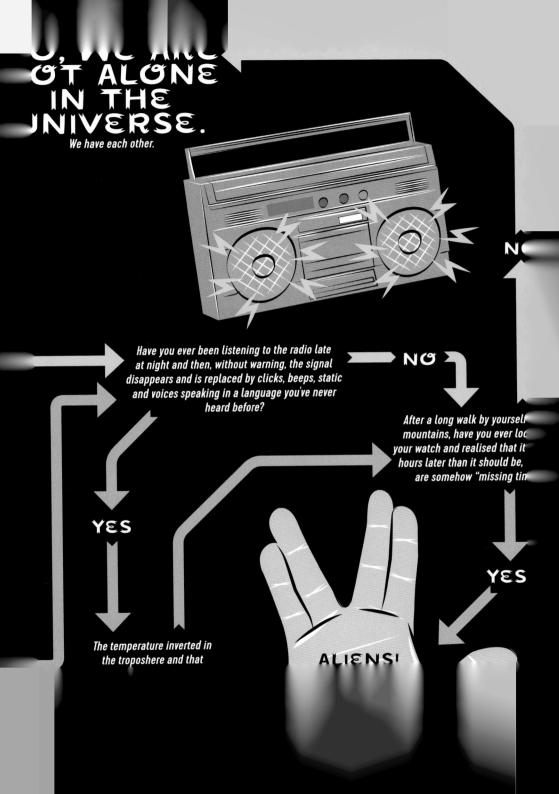

NO, WE ARE
NOT ALONE
IN THE
UNIVERSE.
We have each other.

NO

Have you ever been listening to the radio late
at night and then, without warning, the signal
disappears and is replaced by clicks, beeps, static
and voices speaking in a language you've never
heard before?

NO

After a long walk by yourself
mountains, have you ever loo
your watch and realised that it
hours later than it should be,
are somehow "missing tim

YES

YES

The temperature inverted in
the troposhere and that

ALIENS!

WHERE SHOULD YOU RUN AWAY TO JOIN?

Alright! Let's blow this popsicle stand. What made you decide to go on the lam?

I uncovered a conspiracy that goes right to the heart of government.

Mounting library fines.

Shouldn't you tell someone about that?

Is there anyone who'll miss you when you're gone?

Do my spouse and children count?

You sound just like my sources.

Does the librarian count?

What have you packed?

What are you hoping to find out there, in the unknown?

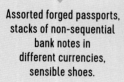

Assorted forged passports, stacks of non-sequential bank notes in different currencies, sensible shoes.

Snorkel, beach towel, bucket and spade.

Danger.

You should run away to join

THE FRENCH FOREIGN LEGION.

Adventure calls your name — adventure, as well as those white circular hats, you know, the ones with the peaks. They still have those hats, right? You should definitely check that out before you sign up.

Seasickness.

Is there anything
holding you back?

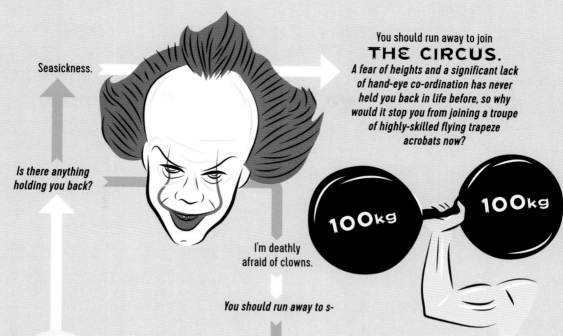

You should run away to join
THE CIRCUS.
*A fear of heights and a significant lack
of hand-eye co-ordination has never
held you back in life before, so why
would it stop you from joining a troupe
of highly-skilled flying trapeze
acrobats now?*

I'm deathly
afraid of clowns.

You should run away to s-

Also crowds, elephants, human canonballs, tiered
seating, those cartoonish weights that Victorian
strongmen used to lift, men in big hats
yelling into cones, sawdust...

Celibacy.

You should
RUN AWAY TO SEA.
*"Worse things have happened at sea", well-meaning relatives have
murmured to you over the years, but you've never quite believed
them. Bad things don't happen at sea, narratively thrilling things
do. Captured by pirates? You put in your time and end up the
captain of a galleon. Shipwrecked? You lose some weight and
become pals with a volleyball. At the very least, you might find
yourself on a ship of lost souls, peeling potatoes by day, smoking
clove cigarettes by night, and never telling another soul about
that book you keep forgetting to take back.*

You should run away to join
A MONASTERY.
*Admittedly, you are slightly concerned that you
would soon tire of the whole married-to-a-deity
situation, but how refreshing would it be to get
a bit of peace and quiet for once?
They probably don't even let you bring
in a phone or anything.*

WHAT FUTURISTIC-INVENTION -THAT-HASN'T-BEEN-INVENTED -YET WOULD REALLY HELP YOU OUT RIGHT NOW?

Is it your job to track down bioengineered androids (despite the fact that you may be one yourself) and you're having trouble getting around your dystopian city where the rich live in literal pyramids and the poor roam the sodden neon streets?

NO

YES

Are you struggling with storage space in your kitchen?

A FLYING CAR.

NO

YES

Have you travelled thirty years forward in time and are now being chased by futuristic punks for some reason?

YES

A HOVERBOARD.

FOOD IN PILL FORM.

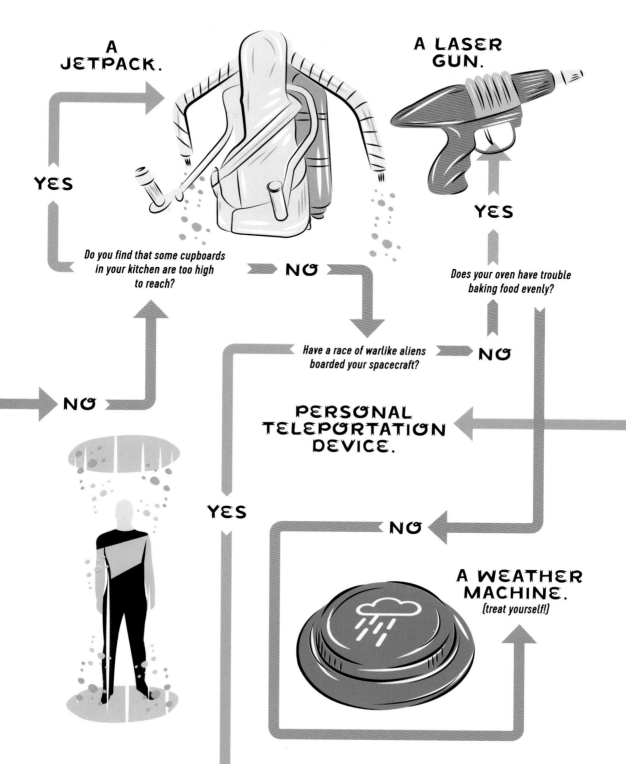

A
JETPACK.

A LASER
GUN.

YES

YES

Do you find that some cupboards
in your kitchen are too high
to reach?

NO

Does your oven have trouble
baking food evenly?

Have a race of warlike aliens
boarded your spacecraft?

NO

NO

PERSONAL
TELEPORTATION
DEVICE.

YES

NO

A WEATHER
MACHINE.
(treat yourself!)

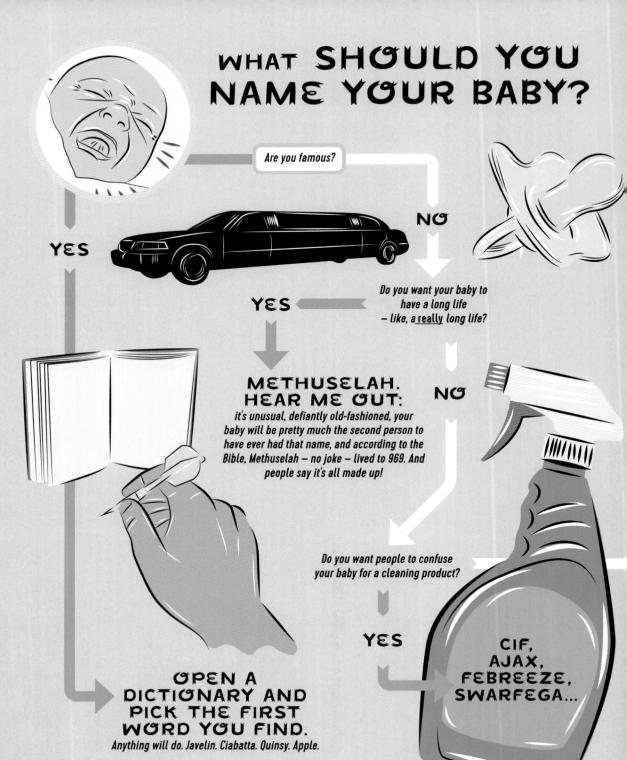

WHAT SHOULD YOU NAME YOUR BABY?

Are you famous?

NO

YES

Do you want your baby to have a long life – like, a _really_ long life?

YES

NO

METHUSELAH. HEAR ME OUT:
it's unusual, defiantly old-fashioned, your baby will be pretty much the second person to have ever had that name, and according to the Bible, Methuselah – no joke – lived to 969. And people say it's all made up!

Do you want people to confuse your baby for a cleaning product?

YES

CIF, AJAX, FEBREEZE, SWARFEGA...

OPEN A DICTIONARY AND PICK THE FIRST WORD YOU FIND.
Anything will do. Javelin. Ciabatta. Quinsy. Apple.

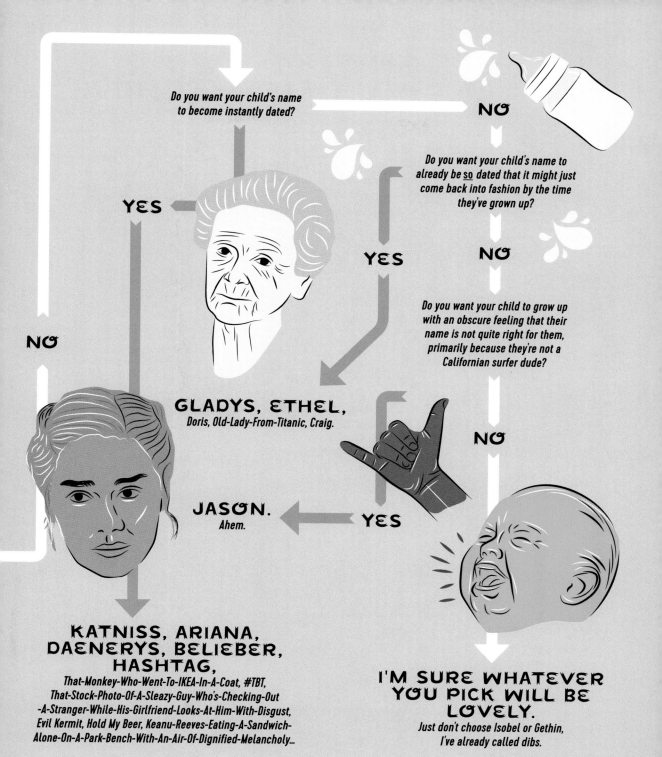

Do you want your child's name to become instantly dated?

NO

YES

NO

Do you want your child's name to already be _so_ dated that it might just come back into fashion by the time they've grown up?

YES

NO

Do you want your child to grow up with an obscure feeling that their name is not quite right for them, primarily because they're not a Californian surfer dude?

GLADYS, ETHEL,
Doris, Old-Lady-From-Titanic, Craig.

JASON.
Ahem.

NO

YES

KATNISS, ARIANA, DAENERYS, BELIEBER, HASHTAG,
That-Monkey-Who-Went-To-IKEA-In-A-Coat, #TBT, That-Stock-Photo-Of-A-Sleazy-Guy-Who's-Checking-Out -A-Stranger-While-His-Girlfriend-Looks-At-Him-With-Disgust, Evil Kermit, Hold My Beer, Keanu-Reeves-Eating-A-Sandwich- Alone-On-A-Park-Bench-With-An-Air-Of-Dignified-Melancholy...

I'M SURE WHATEVER YOU PICK WILL BE LOVELY.
Just don't choose Isobel or Gethin, I've already called dibs.

SHOULD YOU USE
THE TIME MACHINE
YOU JUST FOUND ON THE STREET?

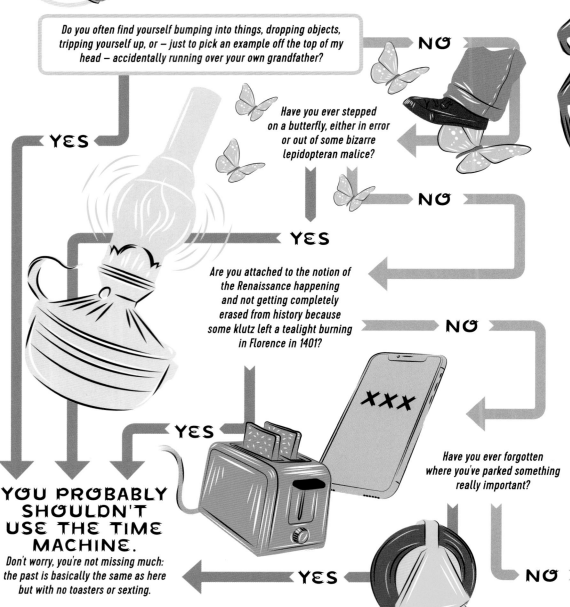

Do you often find yourself bumping into things, dropping objects, tripping yourself up, or – just to pick an example off the top of my head – accidentally running over your own grandfather?

NO

YES

Have you ever stepped on a butterfly, either in error or out of some bizarre lepidopteran malice?

NO

YES

Are you attached to the notion of the Renaissance happening and not getting completely erased from history because some klutz left a tealight burning in Florence in 1401?

NO

YES

Have you ever forgotten where you've parked something really important?

YOU PROBABLY SHOULDN'T USE THE TIME MACHINE.

Don't worry, you're not missing much: the past is basically the same as here but with no toasters or sexting.

YES

NO

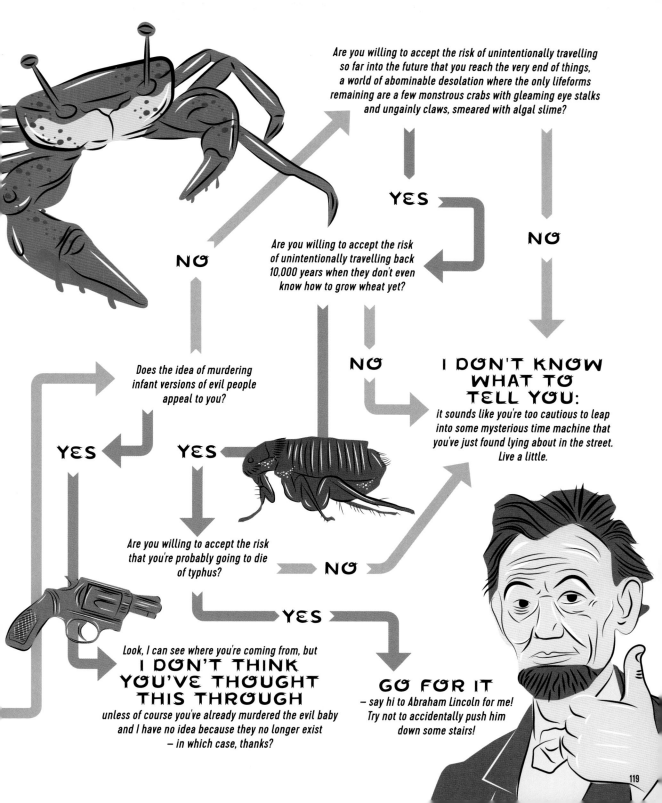

Are you willing to accept the risk of unintentionally travelling so far into the future that you reach the very end of things, a world of abominable desolation where the only lifeforms remaining are a few monstrous crabs with gleaming eye stalks and ungainly claws, smeared with algal slime?

YES

NO

NO

Are you willing to accept the risk of unintentionally travelling back 10,000 years when they don't even know how to grow wheat yet?

Does the idea of murdering infant versions of evil people appeal to you?

NO

I DON'T KNOW WHAT TO TELL YOU:
it sounds like you're too cautious to leap into some mysterious time machine that you've just found lying about in the street. Live a little.

YES

YES

Are you willing to accept the risk that you're probably going to die of typhus?

NO

YES

Look, I can see where you're coming from, but
I DON'T THINK YOU'VE THOUGHT THIS THROUGH
unless of course you've already murdered the evil baby and I have no idea because they no longer exist – in which case, thanks?

GO FOR IT
– say hi to Abraham Lincoln for me! Try not to accidentally push him down some stairs!

119

WHAT DO YOU HAVE TO LOOK FORWARD TO NEXT YEAR?

Which season is your favourite?

SPRING.

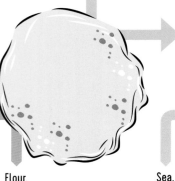

SUMMER.

Flower or flour?

Sea or see?

Flower.

Flour.

Sea.

See.

Walking down a street and being
SHOWERED BY FALLING CHERRY BLOSSOMS.

The notion that every single year there's an entire day just based around the
THE CONCEPT OF PANCAKES.

THE SMELL OF YOUR SKIN
after you've been in the sea.

Being in a place so remote that you can
SEE EVERY STAR IN THE SKY.

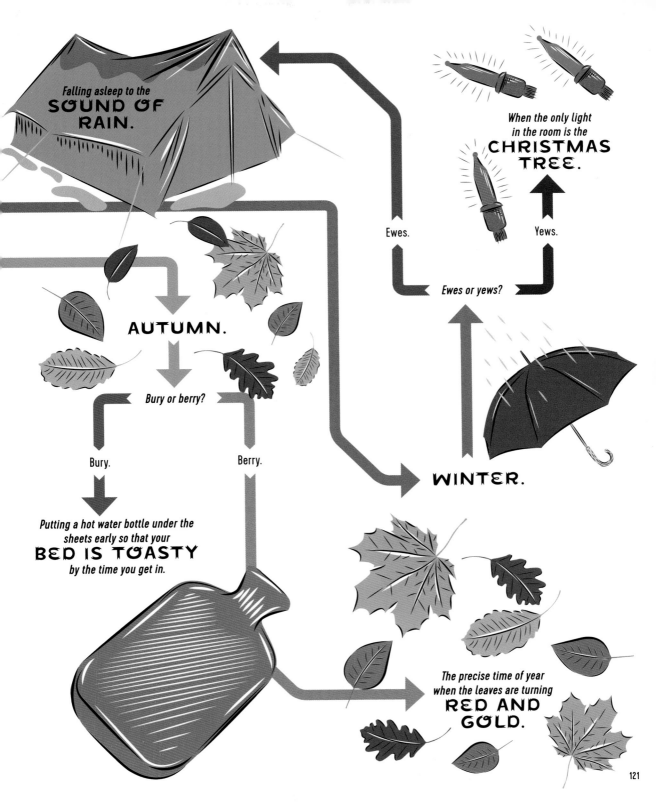

Falling asleep to the
SOUND OF RAIN.

When the only light
in the room is the
CHRISTMAS TREE.

Ewes.

Yews.

Ewes or yews?

AUTUMN.

Bury or berry?

Bury.

Berry.

WINTER.

Putting a hot water bottle under the
sheets early so that your
BED IS TOASTY
by the time you get in.

The precise time of year
when the leaves are turning
RED AND GOLD.

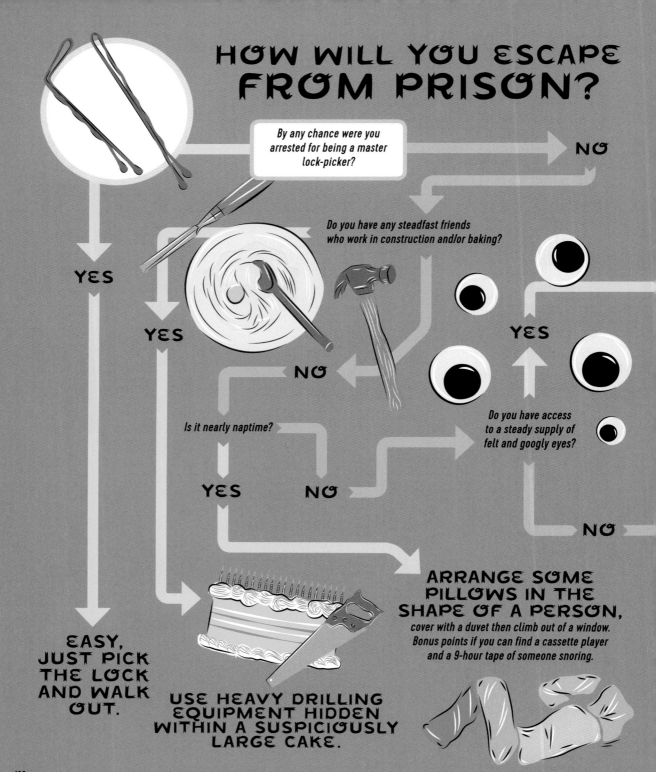

HOW WILL YOU ESCAPE FROM PRISON?

By any chance were you arrested for being a master lock-picker?

NO

YES

Do you have any steadfast friends who work in construction and/or baking?

YES

NO

YES

Do you have access to a steady supply of felt and googly eyes?

Is it nearly naptime?

YES

NO

NO

EASY, JUST PICK THE LOCK AND WALK OUT.

USE HEAVY DRILLING EQUIPMENT HIDDEN WITHIN A SUSPICIOUSLY LARGE CAKE.

ARRANGE SOME PILLOWS IN THE SHAPE OF A PERSON, cover with a duvet then climb out of a window. Bonus points if you can find a cassette player and a 9-hour tape of someone snoring.

STAGE A PUPPET SHOW

as an elaborate distraction/genuine attempt to cheer up your fellow inmates.

EXIT

Distract the guards by TEACHING THEM HOW TO TIE COMPLICATED NAVAL KNOTS.

As they're busying themselves with the double bowline, head to the prison laundry, construct a makeshift rope out of bedsheets and use it to scale the walls.

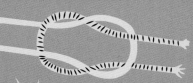

YES

Do you know anyone on the outside who might be willing to loan you their collection — or even just one, really — of very long ropes?

NO

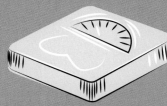

NO

Did you fall into a life of crime in a misguided effort to supplement your struggling illusionist career?

Have you lost weight recently? I mean, <u>a lot</u> of weight?

YES

NO

Are you willing to play a dastardly long con?

YES

Turn sideways, take a deep breath and **SLIDE BETWEEN THE BARS.**

Depart your prison cell through a **CONCEALED TRAP DOOR,** leaving your racy assistant standing in your place. Hire a new assistant.

YES

WAIT 5-10 YEARS

until your sentence is completed and then sneak out the front gates as they release you. The perfect crime.

WHAT SHOULD YOU DO AFTER READING THIS BOOK?

Phew, you made it.
I'm glad we're together in this.
How do endings make you feel?

EXHAUSTED.

INVIGORATED.

TREPIDATIOUS.

GO FOR A WALK.

Don't put off joy. The sun is shining, or else it will be soon.
Should you take an umbrella?
The "Should you take an umbrella?" flow chart might have helped, except the author scrapped that one at the last minute (sorry). It's all too late now, anyway. You're like a shark: constantly moving forward, a statistically low risk to swimmers, you shed 35,000 teeth during your lifetime, and you are always somewhat cold.

RE-READ THIS BOOK.

On your next go around, pretend to be an entirely different person – a part-time cobbler, say, or a disgraced anteater – and see what answers you get. To get the full experience I'd strongly recommend buying another copy.

DO NOTHING.

Not forever, obviously, but how pleasurable is it to finish a book and luxuriate in the sense of completion, reflecting on everything you've read?
This is true even when the reading material happens to be clearly ridiculous. You put the book down, reach for your phone, then stop yourself.
"No," you think, "I'm just going to sit here for a little while, alive in the world."

CONTEMPLATIVE.

HOPEFUL.

THIRSTY.

READ SOMETHING ELSE.

Books, eh? You'll never get to the end of them, even if every writer quit the profession to catch up on their correspondence. Books books books books, books forever, books all the way down, books until you're dead.

DRINK SOME WATER.

Couldn't hurt, could it.

INDEX

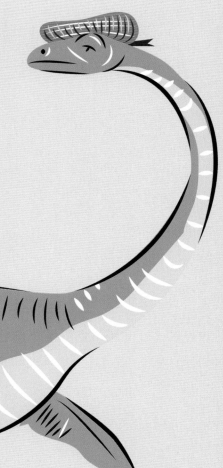